Entrepreneur MAGAZINE'S POCKET GUIDES

How to Sell AUTOMOTIVE PARTS AND ACCESSORIES on eBay

Entrepreneur Press and J.S. McDougall

Entre
Pr

Editorial Director: Jere L. Calmes
Cover Design: Beth Hansen-Winter
Production and Composition: Eliot House Productions

This publication is designed to provide accurate and authoritative information in regard to the subject matter covered. It is sold with the understanding that the publisher is not engaged in rendering legal, accounting or other professional services. If legal advice or other expert assistance is required, the services of a competent professional person should be sought.

Library of Congress Cataloging-in-Publication Data
McDougall, J. S.
How to sell automotive parts and accessories on eBay/by Entrepreneur Press and J.S. McDougall.
p. cm.
ISBN-13: 978-1-59918-080-9 (alk. paper)
ISBN-10: 1-59918-080-4
1. Automobiles—Equipment and supplies—Internet marketing. 2. eBay (Firm) I. McDougall, J. S. II. Entrepreneur Press.
HD9710.3.A2H69 2007
629.2068'8—dc22 2007001387

Printed in Canada
12 11 10 09 08 07 10 9 8 7 6 5 4 3 2 1

How to Sell
AUTOMOTIVE PARTS AND ACCESSORIES
on
eBay

Other Entrepreneur Pocket Guides include

How to Sell Clothing, Shoes, and Accessories on eBay

How to Sell Collectibles on eBay

How to Sell Computers and Accessories on eBay

How to Sell Toys and Hobbies on eBay

Contents

Appendix

Preface

Think about this: the average American adult spends more than ten hours per week stuck in traffic jams. That's five full workdays every month that a person spends sitting behind the wheel of a stopped car, behind a line of stopped cars, wishing to be somewhere else. To put it in a larger perspective, that time amounts to 480 hours—or 20 full days—every year, just sitting, wishing.

If your daily commute involves hours of idly surfing the radio stations, making unnecessary phone calls, and humming commercial jingles while tapping on your steering wheel, you understand the problem. Traffic jams rattle your nerves and are hard on your engine. They waste your time, gas money, and the precious little patience you have at the end of the workday. Luckily, we're here to suggest several simple solutions. First, you could build an eight-lane freeway from your office to your driveway. Or if you're sick of freeways, you could redesign our societal structure and junk the whole urban-suburban thing. Or if you don't have the knack for city planning, you could buy a helicopter, rent a helipad near the office, and fly over the whole mess.

If those options strike you as an overly expensive way to save time getting to work, you have one last option—quitting your job—and it is free. Sure, the bills will keep on coming, and the mortgage won't go away, but the simple act of telling your boss where he can stick his traffic jam won't cost a penny. So what do you do? How is it possible to earn your keep while living in your pajamas? Would you rather work from your back porch and let FedEx fight the traffic? The internet makes it possible.

eBay has more than 204 million registered users worldwide and is growing at breakneck speed. In the last year alone, eBay added nearly 50 million new users. This colossal network of buyers and sellers reaches into nearly every home in the country. eBay sold roughly $52 billion worth of merchandise through its online marketplace last year. That means that the site sold about $1,647 worth of items for its sellers *every second.* With sales like that, you can see why there are more than 724,000 professional sellers who use selling on eBay as their primary or secondary source of income. There is no reason that you cannot join them by selling the items that interest you.

This book will provide you with tips and tools from eBay's auto parts PowerSellers. We cover every step in the process—from registering on eBay to fine tuning your advanced selling strategies. With the information contained in this book, you will be able to create an income for yourself, gain the freedom to work where you like, build your own auto parts business, and travel only when and where you please. Also, once you're up and selling, you will be able to sit happily in your living room, basking in the knowledge that every month you sell thousands of quality auto parts to people who use them to keep their cars running while they sit in traffic jams.

For Nanna

CHAPTER 1

Charting **the Water**

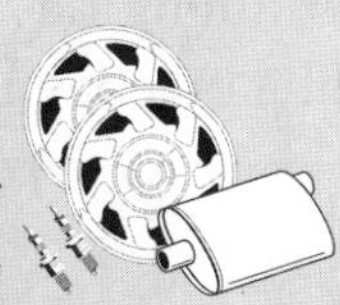

The decision to sell auto parts is a good one. eBay's "Cars, Boats, Vehicles & Parts" category became so popular, and grew so large over the years, that eBay needed to expand the category into eBay Motors—a specialty site dedicated to everything automotive. Clicking the "Cars, Boats, Vehicles & Parts" link on eBay's homepage will take you to eBay Motors. eBay Motors is where buyers can find everything from a 1925 Model T to dashboard lightbulbs for the newest Civic. It sells items for cars, trucks, all-terrain vehicles (ATVs), boats, planes, dirt bikes, and anything else with a motor and steering wheel. eBay Motors alone sells more than $13 billion worth of goods for its sellers every year—or $411 worth of goods every second. Finding a niche in such a vast marketplace can be a lucrative endeavor.

While selling on eBay is a great way to earn money, it is not a get-rich-quick miracle. It requires long hours and a lot of patience. Care must be taken when conducting all your transactions and dealing with bidders. eBay's feedback system is a double-edged sword. It will boast to the world how great a seller you are, and also reveal to the world exactly where you are lagging behind. It takes a lot of work to make and keep buyers happy. Anyone who has ever had a job that deals directly with the public knows this already. If you do not have the time or interest to devote to taking care of the details of doing business, such as getting packages to the UPS Store on time in the middle of a snowstorm, or answering buyer e-mails after a long day of crunching numbers in your cubicle, then selling on eBay is not for you. Your feedback score will suffer, and soon buyers will shy away from your listings. If you're ready and excited for the possibilities eBay presents, however, then you will have a rewarding and profitable experience.

EBAY TIP

Auto parts have a tremendous market on eBay. The second largest store on eBay, Car Parts Wholesale, claims to have 100,000 parts stocked and more than 123,000 happy customers.

PowerSelling vs. Hobby Selling

The first step in selling on eBay is to decide your commitment level to this endeavor. There are two levels of commitment when discussing selling on eBay: hobby seller and PowerSeller. The hobby seller sells casually for extra cash when he finds time in his schedule. The PowerSeller has made selling online his career. The tips found in this book will help both the hobby seller and the PowerSeller become more successful; the initial planning for these two commitment levels is decidedly different. We'll discuss the differences throughout the book, but for now just think carefully about whether you want to depend on selling auto parts on eBay as your only income, or want it to supplement what you're already earning elsewhere.

Both hobby selling and PowerSelling can be fun, exciting, and lucrative. If you're not sure where to begin, plan to start small and grow over time. It's much easier to start selling as a hobby to supplement your job than it is to start selling full time and then grovel for your job back if you decide this career isn't for you.

Anyone who is gung-ho about selling on eBay should plan to start big. Starting small may seem less daunting, but it is often the more difficult road. Having more inventory in the beginning means that your items will appear in buyer searches a larger percentage of the time. Getting started with more capital will help you to have all the appropriate pieces—design, payment systems, communications—in place so that when the higher number of buyers see your items a higher percentage of the time, you'll be able to close the sale more reliably than those sellers who choose to start small.

Competition

As we mentioned earlier, auto parts are immensely popular with eBay buyers. They are also immensely popular with eBay sellers—which means you will find plenty of competition in this category. Be aware that if you plan to reach the coveted PowerSeller status, you have your work cut out for you. Many PowerSellers are busy keeping a careful eye not only on their own businesses, but also on their competition—you.

> **EBAY TIP**
>
> Do numerous searches on eBay for the types of auto parts you would like to sell. Search both active and completed listings. The sellers you find here will become your competition.

The bright side of having a lot of competition is that it provides many opportunities for market research. This is where you should begin your journey to becoming a successful eBay auto parts seller. Know your competition, both on eBay and off. What are their strengths? More importantly, what are their weaknesses? If your competition sells on eBay, find and study their product listings. Are the listings attractive, complete, clear? Read the customer feedback comments. Are buyers complaining about slow shipping, inaccurate descriptions, or poor customer service? Find any faults, and make it your goal to provide better service in these areas.

Your off eBay competition will be more familiar to you. You'll be competing with the national retail chains such as Wal-Mart and Target, along with specialized auto parts stores such as AutoZone and NAPA. Visit these stores and browse their selections. What can you offer that they don't carry? Are you interested in specializing in just one area of auto parts? Can you offer what the stores do at a better price? Make notes of what you find and incorporate them into your product strategy.

Devising a Product Strategy

"Auto parts" is an umbrella-like term covering everything from cartoon license plate brackets to custom racing seats to motorcycle chains. Finding your niche within the category can be quite a task. There are a few things to consider before you begin investing in inventory.

New, Used, or Classic

The eBay Motors "Parts & Accessories" category contains items of all vintages. It has the latest retail in-dash GPS systems, and 1962 VW Beetle taillight lens covers that predate Herbie the Love Bug. You'll need to think about whether you would like to sell new, used, or classic items. Each has its advantages and drawbacks.

New Items. Selling new items in eBay auctions can be challenging. Most bidders search through auctions expecting to find a bargain. In fact, most new items in auctions sell for only around 20 percent below retail price. Above that, bidders decide it is worth it to buy the item locally for a few bucks more. So profit margins can be slim.

Selling new items in an eBay Store, however, is another matter. Auto parts stores abound on eBay where prices are retail and items are squeaky clean. Once bidders move past auctions and become shoppers in a seller's eBay Store, expectations shift. No longer are prices fluid. They are fixed prices on fixed inventories. Now, normal retail prices are no longer seen as an offense; they are expected. Many PowerSellers sell more than 90 percent of their items from their eBay Stores, simply because the fixed prices allow them to guarantee suitable profits on every sale.

One major advantage to selling new auto parts is the ease of sourcing items. New items have active product lines. They are still in production, and moving along traditional product channels from manufacturer, to distributor, to wholesaler, to retailer, to end consumer. Finding and buying items at any point along this chain can be easier and less time consuming than scouring 1,000 salvage yards looking for a steering wheel for a 1960 Saab GT750. See Chapter 4 for more about finding inventory.

Demand for new items depends, of course, on the item. Just as it is in the rest of the retail world, items that don't catch a buyer's attention simply don't sell. Be sure you have done your homework and are ready to capitalize on the market's trends and mainstays.

USED ITEMS. Selling used, nonclassic items has some significant advantages over selling new items. For one, used items are less expensive to buy. Salvage yards, used car lots, and local auctions are often full of old vehicles that can provide good parts. If you don't mind scrubbing off years of oil buildup, or tagging what piece goes where, selling used auto parts may be for you.

In order to make a profit selling used auto parts for low prices, you'll need to either sell thousands of parts for ubiquitous car models, or specialize in parts for just a few classics. If you don't mind high turnover being the driving force behind high revenues, the first option might be a good way to go. Selling classic items may be your best choice, however, if you have a passion that leads you toward specializing in hard-to-find parts for out-of-production classic cars; such parts could command a healthy premium.

EBAY TIP

One of the disadvantages to selling used parts is that you won't have the luxury of a steady supply. In order to keep your shelves stocked, you will need to be constantly searching for new inventory.

CLASSIC ITEMS. The main advantage to selling classic items is that there seems to be a collector in the world for anything. If you're considering selling classic items or collectibles, chances are that you're a collector in some form already. Most anything considered to be classic is in high demand, and therefore can produce high profits. Established franchise models, such as the Porche 911, the VW

Station Wagon bus, and the Ford Mustang all have devout followers who gobble up related items, whether it's a keychain or a hood emblem.

Expertise is a must for anyone dealing in classic items. Bidders and buyers expect an item's seller to be able to answer their questions. For example, if you're selling classic logo emblems, you'll be expected to know what model car it was used on, and for which years. You'll also need to know where it fits in the evolution of the logo, and what it is worth to collectors. Selling classic parts and collectibles is a good idea if you have a driving passion for a specific vehicle or vehicle manufacturer in history. If you're unsure about the idea, however, consider selling new auto parts.

Sell What You Know

As mentioned briefly above, you should sell items you know something about. This is not simply for the sake of being able to answer your customers' questions, but also for yourself. There are two main problems with basing your decision about what to sell solely on potential profitability. First, you could end up choosing a product about which you know nothing. This will be bad for customer relations and business in general. Second, if you don't take into account your own personal interest in the products, you'll likely lose your passion for the business over time. Selling on eBay represents a giant opportunity for you to begin something you will be passionate about. Aside from owning your own schedule and income, you should also be excited to go to work in the morning. What could be better than getting up every day and going into the office to play with your favorite things? There are so many potential niches within the auto parts category that anyone should be able to find one that appeals more than others. Speed enthusiasts could sell high-performance motorcycle exhaust systems; the off-road crowd could sell after-market racks and luggage for ATVs; car buffs could sell custom accessories such as skull shifters, chrome hub caps, and leopard-print seat cushions. There's no end to the possibilities. Assess your own passions and plan accordingly.

Recognizing Opportunity

One of the keys to building a profitable business is to evaluate each possible selling opportunity that comes along. While deciding what type of auto parts to sell, it is important to consider feasibility along with profitability and your own passions. For example, say you are passionate about fuzzy dice, and you see that they are selling well on eBay. Do you have the room to store and ship thousands of fuzzy dice every month? Or perhaps you are passionate about—and already have a basement full of—Mercedes keyrings. Are they selling on eBay? Be sure to allow yourself the time to consider every angle of proper product selection before sinking money into inventory.

One more thing to consider when selecting a product line: constant demand vs. shopping trends.

CONSTANT DEMAND. Some items are constantly in demand. These tend to be the parts of popular vehicles that need replacing due to wear over time. Every car, truck, motorcycle, ATV, and dirt bike has parts that wear out, such as oil filters, tires, chains, inner tubes, and air filters. Finding a manufacturer of new after-market parts for the wear parts on any of these vehicles isn't difficult. If you are able to secure a deal with a manufacturer, supply the parts at a price below or comparable to retail, and provide great customer service, you could soon have a booming business. As long as vehicles are on the road, they'll have parts that need replacing.

Also in constant demand are lower prices. Bargain hunters are ubiquitous on eBay. You can sell most anything if you deliver it at prices 20 percent below retail or lower. It can be tricky to sell that far below retail and still turn a profit, but because your operating expenses should be lower than the average auto parts retail outlet, you are likely to have some wiggle room. If this is your chosen route, try to sell in high volume to offset the lower profits per item.

SHOPPING TRENDS. Every once in a while an automotive shopping trend comes along that sends people in droves to their auto parts store. Such trends don't occur as frequently as in some other markets, such as mobile phones or MP3 players, but the automotive industry has its share. For example, remember when the Yosemite Sam adorned the mud flaps of every other truck? Or how about when Calvin began urinating on a variety of manufacturers' names? More recently, the Tom-Tom navigation systems and various iPod audio accessories have been popping up in cars and trucks everywhere.

Try to seek out upcoming trends and capitalize on them. Watch for product releases, big marketing pushes, and even in-movie product placement to find out what's coming next to automotive trends. It could be apparel, audio accessories, floormats, or stickers. All of the above would do well in an eBay Store if timed correctly.

Now that you've gotten a brief overview of the eBay auto parts landscape, it's time to meet some PowerSellers who have mastered that landscape. They have spent years building their businesses and have graciously agreed to help you do the same. So get excited to get started; this is where the journey begins.

CHAPTER 2

Meet the **PowerSellers**

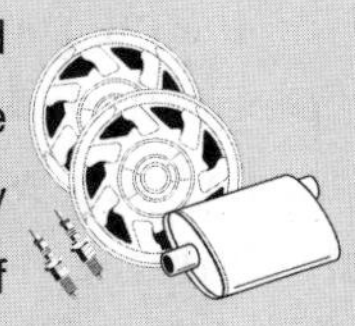

To help bring to light the opportunities and obstacles of selling auto parts on eBay, we have interviewed some top sellers in the eBay Motors Parts and Accessories category. Each of the sellers profiled below has attained PowerSeller status.

To become a PowerSeller, a seller must:

- Have been an active seller on eBay for more than 90 days.
- List at least four items per month for three consecutive months.
- Reach a feedback level of at least 100 with a 98 percent positive rating.
- Generate at least $1,000 per month for at least three months in a row.

Here are brief descriptions of the PowerSellers and their businesses. You will also find helpful tips from these sellers in the chapters ahead.

sumofallparts

Joseph Browning, of sumofallparts, has found great success on eBay, even though his arrival on the site was not ushered in with good omens. His decision to sell on eBay came shortly after his friend was in a motorcycle accident. The friend survived, but the motorcycle was not so lucky—which left Browning and his friend with a broken hunk of a vehicle. They had heard about a site where they might be able to sell off the motorcycle parts, and decided to dismantle what was left of the motorcycle and have a go at it. They auctioned off all the usable parts they could and earned more money selling the pieces than the motorcycle was worth whole. They decided to start a business selling new and used after-market and original equipment manufacturer (OEM) motorcycle parts on eBay under the name Sum Of All Parts. They went live on September 12, 2001.

Since then they have racked up more than 12,000 satisfied customers, with a 99.4 percent positive feedback rating. They have an eBay Store stocked with thousands of parts and accessories for all makes and models of motorcycles, with their focus on the high-performance racing segment. Sum Of All Parts now employs 12 people, full and part time, in its 3,500-square-foot warehouse in Austin, Texas.

Browning credits the store's success to customer service and community support. Employees make a point to personalize all their e-mail correspondence with buyers and even offer a 12-minute email response guarantee during business hours. Browning says his staff puts in 300 hours per week communicating with customers and helping them to find the right part for their sport bike, dirt bike, or ATV. All the store's products are backed by a 30-day 100 percent money-back guarantee—something buyers are still surprised to find on eBay.

With 3,553 happy customers in the last six months, Sum Of All Parts clearly has a strategy for customer care that is working. Visit this great store on eBay (http://stores.ebay.com/sum-of-all-parts-store) when you get the chance.

techchoiceparts

Greg Macintosh, of techchoiceparts, started selling on eBay in 2002 after a friend of his mentioned the success he had been having selling on the site. Macintosh and his business partner had been in the automotive air-conditioning business for many years, selling, rebuilding, and repairing compressors and evaporators in all makes and models of cars and trucks. After hearing about his friend's success, Macintosh picked some popular products from his business, and began selling.

Mactintosh's eBay Store, TechChoice Parts A/C, is stocked with compressors, switches and relays, evaporators, condensers, dashboard A/C controls, and more. Most of the items are for cars and trucks that are now five to seven years old and at the age where original air-conditioning systems break down. All of the products are individually evaluated before they are listed, and many must go through the remanufacturing process, which involves breaking the item down and testing each internal piece for wear, rust, cracks, or damage. Each faulty piece is replaced and retested before the item makes it to eBay.

Even with all the time invested in making sure the company's products work flawlessly, Macintosh still asserts that nearly all of his time is spent interacting with his customers, either on the phone or via e-mail. He finds that his clients are still a little wary when purchasing high-priced items online, and that constant, clear communication is key to building a trusting relationship.

Macintosh and his team at techchoiceparts have earned a 99.9 percent positive feedback rating of 3,078, having sold more than 1,000 of those items in the last 12 months. Their customers credit them with lightning fast shipping, prompt customer service, and accurate descriptions of their products. Clearly, techchoiceparts has put in the hard work necessary to earn its PowerSeller badge. Visit the store at http://stores.ebay.com/techchoice-parts-a-c.

truckpartsaz

David McAnerney, of truckpartsaz, started selling on eBay in August 2000 to help his brother-in-law who owns a truck parts and accessories company. He was unfamiliar with eBay when he first took the job, but found that the site's tutorials walked him through the basics well enough to get some listings up. McAnerney has learned his stuff and is now a PowerSeller in the Parts & Accessories category. Instead of attempting to conquer the entire category, he decided to focus on a niche market that he and his family knew something about—interior and body restoration parts for 1947 to 1987 GMC and Chevrolet trucks.

It may seem like a small market, but when multiplied by the millions of eBay buyers, a niche market can create a viable business. McAnerney works out of his house handling the eBay side of the family business, doing the listing, customer care, and invoicing. All the items he sells are packed and shipped by employees back at the shop, leaving him to work when he pleases.

Besides the money, McAnerney enjoys helping people who share his excitement for restoring old trucks. "The coolest part about selling this stuff on eBay," he says, "is when I get an e-mail that is obviously from a young kid who is excited that I was able to get him the right part to fix up his project truck."

Excitement and knowledge about his products have earned McAnerney and truckpartsaz a 99.9 percent positive feedback rating, and a legion of faithful, truck-restoring followers. Visit the store at: http://stores.ebay.com/truckparts-chevy-gmc-truck-parts.

mvp-imports

Frank Ponte and the people at MVP Imports have been servicing Volvos and selling Volvo parts for more than 30 years. MVP Imports is a Volvo specialty shop in Orange, New Jersey that sells and installs Volvo lamps, lenses, lights, grills, and hubcaps. Ponte began selling on eBay in 2000 with a few turn signals and taillights from his store's stock. He made some profit, so he bought more stock and listed more items, bringing in more profit. Recognizing that he had stumbled onto an opportunity on eBay, he decided to try to capture the Volvo lighting niche market within the Parts & Accessories category.

Since Ponte had been in the Volvo accessory business for a while, he already had established relationships with lamp and lens manufacturers. He had the luxury of knowing at the outset that his product sources were reliable. It was this knowledge that allowed him to so quickly open his appropriately named eBay Store, Volvo Lamps.

Today that eBay Store is stocked with lighting products for more than a dozen models of Volvos. Ponte also sells the occasional hubcap, or hubcap set, and grill. He has four employees and works constantly out of his house and warehouse. He says the job requires that he be on-the-go 24 hours a day, 7 days a week, but that he really enjoys the thrill of competition.

His hard work is paying off. He and his team have earned a 99.9 percent positive feedback rating over six years and thousands of sales. Ponte knows what it takes to find and conquer a lucrative niche market on eBay. Visit his store at http://stores.ebay.com/VOLVO-LAMPS.

swedeng

Crystal Conway is the Used Parts Division manager at Swedish Engineering in Ann Arbor, Michigan. She is responsible for running many aspects of the company's used parts division, but chief among her responsibilities is managing the company's eBay sales. Like Ponte of MVP Imports, Swedish Engineering has been in the Volvo parts and accessories business for more than 30 years. But unlike MVP Imports, it doesn't sell new items direct from the manufacturer. Conway and her team sell used parts from used or damaged Volvos that they dismantle. They find that reclaiming perfectly good parts from otherwise unusable cars is a great way to earn money while providing buyers with less expensive options for repairs and cutting down on landfill waste.

Conway works at the shop with the rest of Swedish Engineering's employees, though she admits that she could manage her eBay duties from anywhere. She doesn't need to spend much of her time interacting with customers because she makes a point to create complete product descriptions and provide part numbers, photos, and model information. This frees her to attend to her other duties at the shop.

Conway has earned a 99.5 percent positive feedback rating and a PowerSeller badge. She is enjoying her eBay experience and is impressed with eBay's ability to sell products. She credits her success to great word of mouth about Swedish Engineering around the local community, but says that even "word of mouth can't travel as fast as the internet. Everybody knows eBay." Visit Conway's eBay Store at http://stores.ebay.com/swedish-engineering-volvo-parts.

> **EBAY TIP**
>
> Look for each of these PowerSellers through eBay's "Find a Member" search. Studying their stores and item listings will provide you with a good example of how to set up your eBay business.

With the information in the chapters ahead, you'll learn to build a business to the level of those described by the PowerSellers above. So get excited, and read on. A successful auto parts store is closer than you think!

CHAPTER 3

The Logistics

Registering for an eBay account is painless. eBay has done a great job making the process straightforward. Still, while it may be technically easy, there are some steps that require careful consideration.

Registration

To begin the process, click the "register" link on eBay.com's main page. You will see a progress bar across the top of the page that shows the three steps in the registration process: "Enter Information," "Choose User ID & Password," and "Check Your E-mail." You will also see a link for "Live Help" at the top of the page. Clicking this link will pop up a little chat window that connects you with a member of the eBay customer service team. If you get stuck during the registration process, or have a question, click this link for help.

Enter Your Information

Enter your personal information into the appropriate text boxes on this page. Be sure to double check your information for accuracy, as it will be used when you conduct business and people need to trust that it is correct.

User Agreement and Privacy Policy

Most people never take the time to read the User Agreements or Privacy Policies of the sites they join. In most cases, this practice in harmless. But in this case, we strongly suggest you read through eBay's User Agreement. It states, in no uncertain terms, the infractions that will get you kicked out of the eBay community and banned from selling on the site. Not all of the infractions are obvious, and some make it quite conceivable that an unsuspecting new user could break one of them relatively easily. Realizing down the road that you have failed to abide by eBay's User Agreement can put an immediate end to your income. It has happened to unsuspecting sellers many times. Please read the User Agreement. Below are some forbidden actions that often trip up new users, with our comments.

While using the site, you will not:

- Post content or items in an inappropriate category or areas on the site. (With something as simple as a missed click of the mouse, a user could mistakenly post an item to an inappropriate category. Be sure to double check.)
- Manipulate the price of any item or interfere with other user's listings. (It is tempting and easy to bid on your own items to boost the sale price, but the practice is strictly forbidden.)
- Distribute or post spam, chain letters, or pyramid schemes. (When the excitement of owning a new business strikes, many new users are tempted to contact as many people as possible to advertise their services. It may not seem so at the time, but this is spamming. It is not allowed through eBay's e-mail forms, in the discussion boards, or from any other contact information collected from eBay's site.)

eBay's User Agreement also contains a very clear Content License clause, which states:

> *When you give us content, you grant us a nonexclusive, worldwide, perpetual, irrevocable, royalty-free, sub-licensable (through multiple tiers) right to exercise the copyright, publicity, and database rights (but no other rights) you have in the content, in any media known now or in the future. (We need these rights to host and display your content.)*

In other words, don't post the text of your upcoming novel as the description of an item, because once you do, eBay owns it.

In addition to these points, there are other important facets of the User Agreement that should be known to every seller. Be sure to read it.

Choose User ID and Password

Choosing the right User ID is important for all sellers, as it will be how people identify you and your business on eBay. Casual sellers have the luxury of considering a variation of their own name as a User ID, while more ambitious sellers do not. The User ID of your eBay business should be short, memorable, easily pronounced, and appropriate for your product line, yet leave room for later growth. For example, a seller of on-dash GPS systems should choose a name that identifies the business as a seller of GPS systems, but doesn't rule out growth into selling automobile DVD players, games systems, and touch screens. "AutoGPS" would be a poor choice, while "HighTechAutoSystems" would serve the seller better down the road.

You may be asked to confirm your identity by entering a credit or debit card number. This is a safety measure to ensure you are over 18 years of age and have a valid mailing address. Your card will not be charged at this time.

> **EBAY TIP**
>
> Choose a User ID that is appropriate for the type of items you will be selling. "Sunshine Rainbow" would not be an appropriate User ID for a seller of oil filters—while adorable, it is misleading.

Check Your E-Mail

Once you have submitted all your information to eBay and chosen your User ID, you will be sent an e-mail asking you to confirm your registration. This e-mail will contain a confirmation code that you will need to enter into eBay's registration confirmation page. This e-mail and confirmation code confirms that the e-mail address you entered is valid and that you have access to it. Follow the instructions in the confirmation e-mail and you will have completed your eBay registration.

In order to begin selling, you will need to register as a seller. Click the "Start Selling" link on the page that comes up when you click the link in your registration confirmation e-mail. You will be asked to enter a credit or debit card number to place on file. This again is just a security measure to confirm your age, name, and address. Your card will not be charged.

You will next be asked to input account and routing information for a checking account. This is a measure eBay takes to ensure that it will be able to collect the seller's fees if the credit or debit card that the seller provides expires. As the last step in this process you must select the method by which to pay your

EBAY TIP

Sometimes spam filters will catch automatically generated e-mails. If you don't receive an e-mail from eBay right after signing up, check your spam folders for new messages.

seller's fees—with the card you've just placed on file, or with money in the bank account.

Account Setup

Now that you've registered, the first order of business is to get your seller's account set up with some necessary information. We will cover a few of the most important items here, but we can't cover everything, so it will be up to you to work your way down the options provided in the "My Account" menu on the left side of your "My eBay" page.

Your "About Me" Page

The content of your "About Me" page is entirely up to you; it gives you the opportunity to tell eBay buyers about yourself, your business, and your products. Most sellers use this page as a place to introduce themselves, put up some photos, lay out their shipping and payment policies, and maybe link to a few of their auctions. If done well, your "About Me" page will show some personality, give buyers a sense of familiarity, and drive sales.

To begin setting up your "About Me" page, log into your account and click "Personal Information" under the "My Account" menu on the left-hand side of the page. On the resulting page, you will be able to edit all the personal information associated with your account. Click "Edit" next to the "About Me" page option.

There are two methods available to you for setting up an "About Me" page: you can use eBay's step-by-step process or you can enter your own HTML code. Writing your own code allows for more customization than the step-by-step process, but is only recommended for sellers who are comfortable writing HTML. This page is not a place where novice coders should cut their teeth. It must have a professional appearance to reflect your business well.

> **EBAY TIP**
>
> It would be worth your while to learn the basics of HTML. There are many good books on the topic, and many free tutorials on the internet. eBay even provides its own tutorial at http://pages.ebay.com/help/sell/html_tips.html.

The step-by-step process will ask for a page title, some text, and some photographs. You can also display your recent sales history, and provide links to helpful web sites. This is the only page on which eBay will allow you to post off eBay links, so do so wisely. Post links to web sites that will be helpful to your buyers. For example, posting a link to a "Finding the Right Headlight Bulb" page will help your buyers get more out of your selection of auto bulbs, but posting a link to photos of your grandmother's lovable dog, Sneezers, will not.

When writing your text for your "About Me" page you should consider including your business mailing address and telephone number. Buyers like to see that you are willing to provide real-world avenues for support. This is an easy way to immediately boost your buyers' confidence. If you work from home, however, and do not yet have a business mailing address and business-specific telephone line, you may not want to list your personal information. There's no limit to the amount of frustration one cranky customer armed with your home telephone number can cause. You should, however, prominently post an e-mail address to receive bidders' questions.

Once you have inserted all your information and configured your options, you then select a layout, preview your page, and submit.

Selling Preferences

From your "My eBay" page, click "Preferences" in the "My Account" menu. You will see a host of options that you should explore and set to your liking. In this preferences panel you will be able to configure almost every facet of your eBay account, from which newsletters you receive to how you accept payments from buyers. This is also the first place you will be asked about PayPal.

PayPal

PayPal enables people to send and receive money online. Having a PayPal account is similar to having a checking account at your local bank. You can deposit money to your PayPal account from your personal bank account, you can withdraw money from your PayPal account in various ways—including electronic transfer to your personal bank account—and you can send money from your PayPal account to any person with an e-mail address.

PayPal was founded in 1998 and it made sending money online so easy that it quickly became the default method buyers used to pay for their eBay purchases. It became so widely used on eBay, in fact, that in late 2002, eBay bought PayPal and got to work further integrating PayPal's services into its own.

Today, PayPal is ubiquitous among eBay auctions. Nearly every seller on eBay has a PayPal account to which they can receive payments from buyers. Not only does PayPal make sending money easier for buyers, it also provides sellers with the ability to accept instant payments, accept major credit cards, and avoid bounced checks and fraudulent money orders. It usually takes only seconds once an auction has ended for full payment from the buyer to be delivered to the seller's PayPal account—making the entire transaction easier for everyone.

> **EBAY TIP**
>
> If you have the ability to create new e-mail addresses for your business, you should create a "PayPal only" address that will be easy for buyers to remember—such as paypal@yourbusiness.com or payments@yourbusiness.com. Protect this e-mail address with rigorous spam filters, as this practice is common, and therefore attracts spammers' attention.

One of the downsides of PayPal is that some buyers find it too risky to submit their sensitive financial information, such as bank account numbers and credit card information, when registering for a PayPal account. They simply refuse to sign up for a PayPal account. This means that making your auctions "PayPal only" will alienate some potential buyers. You should be willing to accept other forms of payment from your buyers such as personal checks or money orders.

Personal Checks and Money Orders

When accepting personal checks and money orders from buyers you should wait a few days to make sure the funds arrive in your account before making the shipment. Sometimes, whether the buyer intends for it to happen or not, personal checks will bounce, leaving you with the hassle of contacting the buyer and collecting payment. Also, a popular method of defrauding sellers on eBay is to send a counterfeit money order for the payment amount. You can and should protect yourself from these scams by waiting to ship any items. Make it clear on each of your item's auction pages that if the buyer intends to with a check or money order, the shipping will be delayed while you wait for funds to clear.

My eBay

The next step to setting up your eBay seller's account is to familiarize yourself with your "My eBay" page. This screen will function as your eBay control panel. It provides up-to-the-minute information concerning all your dealings on eBay: items on which you're bidding; items you're selling; messages from eBay and others in the community; and all your preferences.

Just after you've opened your eBay account, this page will be fairly sparse. But as soon as you become an active eBay community member, this page will burst to life. To help you get that process started, the next chapter will discuss where to search for items to sell in your very own eBay auctions.

CHAPTER 4

Inventory **Resources**

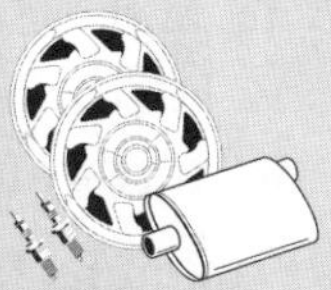

One of the most closely guarded secrets of an eBay PowerSeller is the source of the items they sell. It is hard to get a straight answer out of sellers on the topic, and that's just as it should be. Asking a PowerSeller for their product source secrets is like asking Aunt Berta for her secret cookie recipe—you can ask, but you risk being chased by an aggressive rolling pin.

The PowerSellers we spoke to told us that they continuously search for new sources of items. They search every step of the product's life-chain, from manufacturers to liquidators. And when they find a great source for items, they do all they can to protect and nurture that relationship. A good item source serves as the foundation for building a reliable and profitable business.

As every PowerSeller does, you will also need to do your own research of item sources. The following are some great places to start your search, and a few things to look for in a good source.

New Items

The source of your items depends largely on what you plan to sell. An eBay seller of new high-performance tires will have different sources than a seller of used alternators. So begin with a clear idea of what you want to sell. If you plan to sell new items, make a list of the retailers and manufacturers that you know of in that product line. From that list you can begin to trace your way up and down the product's life-chain to find the best place to buy. For example, if you plan to sell high-performance tires, the product's life-chain will look similar to this:

- manufacturer (Goodyear, Pirelli, Firestone)
- distributor (American Tire Distributors, Kumho Tires, Competition Tire East Inc.)
- wholesaler (Sam's Club, Discount Tire Direct, National Tire Wholesale, eBay Wholesale)
- retailer (Sullivan Tire, Hogan Tire, PepBoys)
- liquidator (liquidation.com, govliquidation.com, etc.)

Pick up the phone and call around to find the sale prices, policies, and restrictions at every step in the chain. Keep in mind that with every successive step in the chain away from the manufacturer, another middleman is added, and the price goes up. So start with the manufacturer and work your way down.

> "The products we sell replace a failed component of an air-conditioning system. Typically, we see the greatest movement on parts where the vehicle is five to seven years old. Sometimes, if there is a design flaw or problem with the original A/C system in a vehicle, we will see sales much earlier in that vehicle's life."
>
> —techchoiceparts

Manufacturers

More often than not, large manufacturers are set up (both physically and financially) to move products down the product life-chain by the truckload, and are unwilling to take the time to sell in smaller quantities or deal with individual sales. This makes buying directly from the manufacturer difficult. Manufacturers occasionally run into the problem of having too much inventory of an older item, however, which can take up valuable space in a warehouse. When you are on the phone with the manufacturer, be sure to ask if they have any overstocked, or dead stock, items that you could help them to liquidate. You'll be doing them a favor by clearing space for their new items, and be getting a good deal on older, but unused, items.

Distributors

When speaking to an item's manufacturer, be sure to ask for the names of its distributors. Call the distributors and ask

> "Folks who are trying to choose what auto maker's parts to sell should first do a little research to see which auto makers have a strong following—which ones have a strong niche that people are attracted to. If you find one, then you know you will have an audience. I believe that being specialized in what you do helps to grow a stronger base and provides a service to folks that they will want to return, and refer, to."
>
> —swedeng

them to become resellers. They may require you to buy in large quantities or pay huge shipping costs, which may or may not work for your business model, but it could provide you with a great source if you can make it work. Be sure to crunch some numbers before you pick up the phone. Also, if you determine that you can, in fact, buy a truckload of fuzzy dice, make sure you have the ability to store, sell, and track that amount of inventory. See more about inventory concerns in Chapter 12.

Wholesalers

Wholesale clubs such as CostCo and Sam's Club should not be overlooked just because they are available to the general shopping public. They fall victim to the same problems of overstocking that many manufacturers run into. You may find deep discounts on desirable items sitting on the warehouse shelves just down the road from you. Just because an item isn't selling in your neck of the woods, does not mean that there isn't high demand for it somewhere among the millions of eBay shoppers. Stick with trusted wholesalers, as most require a membership fee and some could turn out to be scammers.

You can find directories of product wholesalers all over the internet. Be careful using pay services as many directory services are of questionable quality. A great place to try is Worldwide Brands at www.worldwidebrands.com.

> "We sell late model motorcycle performance accessories—almost all new. We chose this because it was something we were interested in. We focus on retail. A large chunk of our revenue comes from liquidation, but our staple is the new retail parts."
>
> —sumofallparts

Retailers

Buying from retailers only makes sense when you can get a deal. Often sellers will find great deals from local retailers by buying up their customer returns. Some large retailers find it cheaper to destroy customer returns than to diagnose, fix, and restock them. So whether an item comes back because it is faulty or simply an unwanted gift, it is destroyed and the retailer absorbs the loss. By buying up customer returns, you get your items at a price significantly lower than retail, and the retailer recoups some loss. Just be aware that customer-returned items are often faulty, and cannot be sold as new or reconditioned items without some repair. It may or may not be worth your time to test and repair items before reselling them.

Another option when sourcing from retailers is to buy their dead stock. Many retailers provide an outlet for their old goods as a way to clean off their shelves and recoup some losses from unsold merchandise. Ask the large retailers in your area if they have such a program.

Liquidators

Many PowerSellers buy their items through liquidation, which is the last step in a new product's life-chain. Items that are never sold to an end consumer are liquidated for a fraction of the retail price, often in bulk. You will find pallets of mostly old and damaged items up for sale—sometimes all mixed together. There are great deals to be had, for sure, but be careful when buying from liquidation companies. Most sell both used and unsold goods from companies that are going out of business, or returned items from retail stores. If you're not careful about what you're buying, and from what company, you might end up stuck with a pallet load of damaged goods that are hard, or impossible, to sell.

Used Items

If you plan to sell used items, you will need to follow a different path to find them than if you were seeking new items. Your path will be a little less formal, a little more fun, and a little closer to home. The disadvantage to selling used items is that steady, reliable sources for quality goods are hard to find. Retail customer-returns, as mentioned above, and liquidation services such as liquidation.com may provide you with a steady stream of items, though it will occasionally be polluted by faulty and unsalable parts.

Direct from Buyers

If you have a knack for dismantling vehicles and know your way around a toolbox, you should consider opening a vehicle dismantling shop. Buying wrecked or old cars for cash can produce some valuable parts for your auctions. The parts of the car that you don't sell on eBay can usually be sold locally to salvage yards or for scrap metal.

Try placing an advertisement in your local paper asking for old, or recently wrecked, vehicles. You've probably seen similar ads in the classifieds saying something akin to "Cash for Cars!" or "We pay cash for your motorcycle!" Place your phone number and e-mail address in the paper with a description of the type of items you're looking to buy, and people will start contacting you. If the response is encouraging, buy one of the vehicles and get started dismantling. As described in Chapter 2, PowerSellers sumofallparts started with a single wrecked motorcycle. Now they have a 3,500-square-foot warehouse and thousands of customers. Imagine what you could do with a fleet of junked motorcycles.

Once your business has grown to a size large enough to handle sizable inventories, consider placing ads in bigger classified markets.

Used Car Auctions

Many used auto parts sellers on eBay find their parts at local used car auctions. Dealers often put their trade-ins up for auction to used car and parts dealers who are willing to fix up, or drag away, older and wrecked cars, trucks, and motorcycles. Buying a classic on a flatbed or a late-model wreck can put some decent parts into your hands. Watch your local paper for auction advertisements, or call a car dealer in town and ask where they auction off trade-ins.

Junk Yards

Don't let the name fool you; there's more than junk in junk yards—especially in newer model cars. When a car has been in an accident, often insurance companies can't justify the cost of having it repaired even though 95 percent of it is untouched. The damaged 5 percent would cost more to repair than what the owner would get for the car if it were sold. Therefore the car is sold by the bank, and the owner is stuck watching his car get towed off to the junk yard. You can buy that untouched 95 percent of the car by contacting the receiving junk yard and striking a deal before the car is dropped in the hopper, or pieced out and sold at the salvage yard. Call the local towing companies to learn where they take damaged cars in your area.

If you are able to get on good terms with the local wreckage and salvage yards, you can secure yourself a steady stream of good parts.

Buy Smart

Now that you've got a few good places to begin your hunt for auto parts to sell, you should begin to think about how to buy smart. Going out and buying all the old auto parts, new auto parts, or collectibles you can find will not produce a profitable business. It will fill your basement and empty your bank accounts. Before you begin buying, you must first find out what items are selling, and at what price. Then, once you've got an idea of what will fly off the shelf and what will collect dust, you can take your knowledge and begin searching in the places listed earlier for the best-selling stuff, at the prices that will make you a profit.

The first place to begin is on eBay itself. Do a search of completed auctions, under the "Advanced Search" link on any page, for items similar to what you would like to sell. Take note of their final sale price, the number of bids they received, and the number of listings for such items. Consider something that received eight or more bids to be a "hot item," meaning that there is significant demand for it and the market could bear more like it for sale. If you find multiple completed listings for an item, each of which has eight or more bids, you've found something worth selling. Your task then becomes to find that item, or the parts to build such an item, at a price that will enable you to make a profit when you sell at the average sale price of the items in your search.

If you find an item that is heavily in demand and are able to list hundreds of that particular item, the average sale price

> "We sell two conditions of product: remanufactured and new. For remanufactured products we have a network of core suppliers where we purchase old cores that were removed from wrecked vehicles. For new products, we have large companies, both OEM manufacturers and aftermarket manufacturers, that we source from."
>
> —techchoiceparts

will plummet, leaving you with little, if any, profits and a flooded market. Introduce your products slowly. There is a delicate balance of supply and demand, especially in the microcosm of an eBay category. Increase the number of your listings while keeping an eye fixed on the dropping average sale price of your products. Experiment with the balance between items sold per month and average sale price per item. You will find a point of maximum profitability.

If the item you're considering selling has many listings with less than eight, or zero, bids, you should consider either a different item or a new approach to selling that item. The harsh reality is that not everything you want to sell will sell. If your dream is to sell rusted heaps of Renault parts, you're likely to be disappointed.

There are many free and commercial tools available to help a person decide what to begin selling. eBay even has some of its own. See Chapter 10 for helpful product research tools.

CHAPTER 5

Listing **Items**

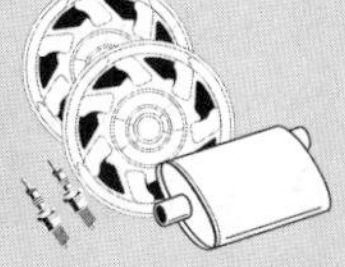

Finally, it is time to begin selling. This chapter will fill you in on the best ways to get your auto parts listed, seen, and sold. eBay is best known for its auctions, but it provides other ways to sell as well. I'll begin by explaining how to list your items in an eBay auction; I'll then describe eBay Stores and Fixed Price Listings—both of which provide great opportunities for sellers to move more auto parts.

Auctions

To begin selling, click the "Sell" tab at the top of the main eBay page. Then click the "Sell Your Item" button. Here you will be presented

QUALIFYING TO SELL

To qualify to sell with Buy It Now prices, a seller must:

- Achieve a feedback score of at least ten.
- Verify their contact information using the ID Verify service ($5 fee).
- Have a PayPal account, achieve a feedback score of five and accept PayPal as a payment method.

with a few options, if you qualify. If you have your eBay Store set up already, and you qualify to list items with "Buy It Now" prices, then you will be shown three options:

1. Sell item at online auction
2. Sell in store inventory
3. Sell at fixed ("Buy It Now") price.

For now, choose sell item at online auction.

Categories

You will be presented with a large list of item categories from which to choose. For the purposes of selling auto parts, the appropriate category for your auction is Parts & Accessories.

Before continuing with Parts & Accessories, take a moment to browse through the lengthy list of eBay top-level categories. You might come across a category that strikes your fancy, one that could lead you to another business opportunity. Who knows? That dusty box in the attic of Great-Grandma's scary stuffed bear collection could fetch a hefty paycheck in the lesser-known Dolls & Bears category.

Once you have clicked Parts & Accessories, scroll down to select a second category for your auction if you wish. Choosing a second category will increase traffic to your listing, and could ultimately raise your final sale price. Don't be tempted, however, to list your item in an inappropriate second category just for the sake of increasing traffic. Listing auctions in inappropriate categories violates the eBay User Agreement and comes with harsh penalties. In most cases, one category is sufficient.

Subcategories

Now you must select a more specific subcategory of the top-level Parts & Accessories category. The subcategory you choose will depend on the item you're selling. You will be presented with a number of interactive menus that will help you narrow your category choice to a specific subcategory. Choose, in every menu, the description that best fits your item. The menus will stop expanding once you have reached the most specific subcategory possible.

Having these specifics helps eBay place your item into a category where it will be best found by buyers searching for your item. By choosing these subcategories carefully and correctly you will improve your item's chances of being shown to the most interested buyers. Therefore, the item's chances of being sold, and of being sold at a good price, partly depend on your selections here.

For example, say that a fictional seller, Duncan, has a large inventory of classic Triumph motorcycle parts that he'd like to put up for auction. He would select Motorcycle Parts in the first menu and then the most appropriate option, British and European, in the second menu. The appropriate third option would depend on the specific item Duncan chose to list here. Say he chose to begin by selling his refurbished voltage regulators because he knew that due to Triumph's notoriously short-lived stock electrical systems, they're sure to be in high demand. In the third menu, he would select Electrical Components.

Below the interactive menus, you will again be presented with the opportunity to choose a second top-level category. If you wish to choose another category, click "continue."

Prefilled Information

For many items from major manufacturers, eBay will present you with an option to use its "Prefilled Information." This helpful feature will automatically fill in your item's auction listing with the manufacturer's default information for that particular model or product. If you happen to be selling an item that eBay has already collected information on, you can take advantage of this option. You won't be offered this option for most auto parts, however.

Standard Listing

Duncan's voltage regulators would not be eligible for the Prefilled Information option, and he would need to provide all the pertinent information about the items by hand. Most of the items you put up for auction will need to be listed in a similar way. Once you skip the Prefilled Information option, you will be presented with the page where you insert the item's title and description.

Title and Description

The importance of writing an effective title and description cannot be understated. In Chapter 7, we will go into detail about what constitutes an effective title and description. But for the purpose of this logistics chapter, we'll give you a brief overview.

Item Title

An auction title is limited to 55 characters, with a character being any letter, number, symbol, or space. The primary function of the title is to clearly state for bidders exactly what the item is that's up for auction. The secondary function of the title is to provide eBay's search program with the keywords it will use to display your auction item in user searches. Balancing these two functions, while remaining under the 55 character limit, can be tricky. We'll provide you with some tips on how best to do this in Chapter 7.

Item Subtitle

If you have a hard time fitting all the necessary information into your item's title, you can purchase the use of a subtitle for 50 cents. The item subtitle has the same limit of 55 characters that the item title has, but the text in the subtitle is not included in eBay's search program. So be sure to fit all the critical search terms into the main title because any text you enter into the subtitle field will only serve to provide additional information to bidders.

PowerSellers sometimes use the subtitle to advertise additional noncritical information about the auction, such as low shipping charges, or to boast about their customer feedback score.

Item Specifics

If your item was originally made by a major manufacturer and is a well-known commodity, chances are that eBay will provide you with an opportunity to give specifics. For example, if you're listing a GPS system, you'll be asked to specify the item's brand, type, and condition. For most items you list in this category eBay will only ask that you specifiy the item's condition.

While many types of auto parts have this Item Specifics option available, quite a few do not. Don't be surprised if the item you're listing does not have this option.

Item Description

The auction description allows you more freedom than the title. There is no character limit, and the description box accepts plain text and HTML. Beginning users should use simple plain text format for the first few auctions, just to get the hang of setting up auctions. Plain text will look just like a simple text document. It will suffice as you're getting started, but you will want to become familiar with HTML so that you are able to take advantage of the formatting benefits it provides. For tips on how to use HTML in your listings, click on the "HTML Tips" link below the description text box.

Creating effective and stunning description pages are covered in Chapter 7. For now, you should write out the basic information regarding your item. Include the model number (if available), the condition, the manufacturer, and any other pertinent information. If you are selling used parts, include the model, year, and manufacturer of the vehicle out of which the part was taken. The more information you provide, the less time you'll spend answering e-mails from bidders.

Pricing and Duration

On the next page you will be asked to provide the various prices, auction duration, and photos for your item's listing. There are strategies to each of these pieces of your auction, which will be covered later in the book. Here, the focus is on defining the terminology used on this page.

Starting Price

The auction's starting price is the amount you set to be the minimum opening bid. If your item sells, it will sell for at least the amount you enter here. The safest strategy is to enter the lowest amount you would be willing to accept for the item. See Chapter 6 for more advanced pricing strategies.

Reserve Price

Setting a reserve price is optional. If one is set, the amount entered here will act as a safety net for sellers. If bidding does not reach the amount you set for the reserve price, you are not obligated to sell your item. When a reserve price is set, bidders are notified on the auction's page, though the amount of the reserve price is hidden to encourage bidding.

Buy It Now Price

The Buy It Now price, or BIN, is a price you can offer to buyers who might want to forego the bidding process and purchase the item immediately. Once a bidder chooses to pay your BIN price, the auction ends. Setting a BIN price is a good idea as it opens up your item to a new market of convenience buyers who do not like to participate in bidding, and are happy to pay a higher price to receive the item sooner.

Donate Percentage of Sale

eBay's Giving Works program allows you to dictate whether or not you would like to donate a portion of the item's ultimate sale price to charity, and, if so, what percentage. If you choose to donate some of your proceeds to charity, eBay will present you with hundreds of nonprofit organizations from which to choose. Once you select an organization from the list and choose the percentage of the sale price you would like to donate, eBay will handle the rest.

Duration

Seven days is the standard length of an eBay auction. You may choose to list an item for one, three, five, or seven days for the standard listing fee. If you would like your auction to run for ten days, eBay will charge you an extra 40 cents. Most PowerSellers use the standard seven-day auction. An auction is easier to keep track of when you can plan on it ending exactly one week from when you submitted it.

Fixed Price Listings

Technically, a fixed price listing is not an auction because there is no bidding, but such a listing will show up in auction search results. This format allows users to buy and sell items immediately at a set price, with no bidding or waiting. You can sell more than one of an item in a fixed price listing, which saves you time and money in listing fees.

Private Listing

Private listings are available for sellers who require anonymity for their bidders during an auction. During a private auction, bidders' User IDs are not displayed on the auction's page or in the bidding history. Only the seller can view the IDs of the different bidders. Setting up a private auction may be appropriate for high-priced items, or items that are so in demand that a buyer would benefit from remaining anonymous.

Start Time

The day and time that your auction ends depends on when your auction begins and the duration you have set. There are two ways to dictate when your auction will end. First, you can submit your auction at the specific time of day that you would like the auction to end, and, when the duration you have set expires, it will end accordingly. Or, for an additional 10 cents, eBay will allow you to schedule the time your auction will start, thereby freeing you to submit your auction whenever you have time.

Most bidding on any particular auction occurs within the last few minutes. This is because as an auction nears its end, it moves up in eBay's auction list when it is sorted in the default "Time: ending soonest" order. Also, savvy bidders have learned not to place bids early in order to prevent other bidders from outbidding them. Rather, they wait until the final few seconds of an auction to place their maximum bid. This way, they keep the final sale price low and improve their chances of sneaking in the last bid. This practice is called "sniping."

Due to sniping, PowerSellers make a point to end their auctions during eBay's peak traffic times. Auctions that end during peak hours receive substantially more bids due to the higher number of bidders on the site who want to see their auction when it is at the top of the list. As a general rule, Sundays, between 6 P.M. and midnight (EST) tend to be eBay's highest traffic times. There are exceptions, of course, such as Super Bowl Sunday when eBay traffic, and internet traffic as a whole, plummets.

Quantity

eBay allows sellers to post auctions that have one or more items for sale. If you are selling one item only, you will not need to specify a quantity. If you are selling multiple items, there are several ways to do so.

INDIVIDUAL ITEMS. If you wish to sell more than one of an identical item, eBay allows you to specify a quantity for an auction provided you meet one of the following requirements. You must be:

- ID verified.
- or have a feedback rating of 30 or more and have been registered on eBay for more than 14 days.
- or have a PayPal account, accept PayPal payments, and have a feedback score of 15 or higher.

Multiple item auctions work differently than single item auctions. Bidders submit their offered price and the number of items they wish to purchase. The winning bid has the highest total price, which equals the offered price multiplied by the number of items requested. All winning bidders pay the lowest successful offered price.

LOTS. If you would like to sell many items in one bunch instead of piecing them out separately, you can sell them as a single lot. You will need to specify the number of identical items that are in the lot and provide a description of them. Bidders will bid on the lot as a whole instead of for one individual item. The winning bidder takes them all.

ITEM LOCATION. This address should be set to the location from which you do your shipping. It is used by buyers to calculate accurate shipping costs, which many people smartly factor into their bids.

Add Pictures

Pictures are a critical piece of your auction. Bidders like to see the items on which they're bidding, and without photos, items sell poorly, or not at all. eBay provides two methods for placing photos in your auctions: you can use eBay's own Basic Picture Services, or a third-party web host.

EBAY BASIC PICTURE SERVICES. If you choose to use eBay's picture services, your first photo will be included in the listing price. Every additional photo you choose to insert will cost 15 cents. To upload photos using this service, simply click the "Browse" button and locate the appropriate photos on your computer.

YOUR WEB HOSTING. To include a photo for free from a third-party web host, you must first upload the photo to your web server, and then enter the address to that photo into the text field. The address should look something like this: www.your webhost.com/ebay/photos/item1.jpg. If everything is correct, the image will be displayed in your auction.

Listing Designer

To help you spice up your auction description, eBay offers the Listing Designer. For an additional 10 cents, this tool allows you to add colorful borders to your listing and select an attractive photo layout. There are quite a few templates from which to choose, so try to find one that is appropriate for the item being auctioned.

Increased Visibility

eBay provides plenty of options that allow you to set your listing apart from the others. Some are worth the additional cost; some are not.

GALLERY. This option will display a thumbnail image of your item in search results and listings. Studies show that using this feature increases final sale price by as much as 11 percent. It is well worth the 35 cent price.

SUBTITLE. A subtitle provides a good opportunity to present more information about your item to bidders in search results and category listings. It has not been shown to increase sale price or conversion rate, so you must decide whether the extra information this allows you to display is worth the 50 cents.

Bold. You may choose to have your auction's title appear in bold type in search results and listings. Bolding, which costs $1, has been shown to improve final sale price by 7 percent.

Border. Adding a border to your listing is a great way to separate it from other auctions. Select this option and a colorful thin border will be placed around your auction listing in search results and category lists. You can expect this option to boost the final sale price by about 7 percent. A border costs $3, and therefore is only worth the expense on high-priced or important promotional auctions.

Highlight. At $5 a highlight is the most expensive aesthetic upgrade you can purchase for your listing. Adding a highlight will fill in a colorful background behind your auction listing in search results and category lists. When coupled with a gallery photo, this option really makes your listing stand out. Generally, it increases final sale price by as much as 15 percent.

Promote Your Listing on eBay

For high-priced or important promotional auctions, eBay offers sellers the chance to advertise their auctions in different "featured" locations across the site. These options are expensive, so they are best used sparingly to attract bidders into auctions that will either fetch a high price, or funnel bidders via cross-promotion into your eBay Store and other auctions.

FEATURED PLUS! At the top of search result pages, eBay displays featured auctions above the regular search results. For $19.95 you can place your auction in the featured spot above appropriate search results listings. This option, while expensive, increases the final sale price of your item by a whopping 76 percent. This option also does a great job of funneling bidders into your auction, and into your eBay Store.

GALLERY FEATURED. This option is similar to the Featured Plus! option. Instead of featuring your auction title at the top of all search result and listing pages, however, this option will display a thumbnail image of your item's first image along with your auction title at the top of the results page when seen in Gallery view. This option costs $19.95; because it is new to eBay, there is no statistical performance information available yet.

HOME PAGE FEATURED. This option is eBay's biggest promotional opportunity. It is quite expensive at $39.95 for one item, and $79.95 for two or more items, but it provides the chance for your auction to appear on eBay's main home page—one of the internet's most popular sites. This option increases bidding on your item by 58 percent. Again, this is a great promotional tool when used correctly.

Gift Services

If you would like to suggest that your item would make a nice gift for someone, you can select to place a gift icon next to your listing title for 25 cents. You then have the option of advertising the following services: gift wrapping, express shipping, and shipping to a gift recipient instead of the buyer.

Page Counter

A page counter is a basic tool that allows you to see the number of times your auction has been visited. There is no charge to include a counter on your auction page.

Payment Methods

As we mentioned earlier, there are several methods for collecting payment from auction winners. If you have registered for a PayPal account, and indicated in your eBay preferences that you would like to accept PayPal payments from buyers, your PayPal information will appear here. If you have chosen to avoid PayPal, you have several options: money order/cashier's check, personal check, and other/see item description. If you select "Other/See Item Description" you will need to be sure that you state your "other" payment terms in your auction's description.

If you have your own merchant account, you can select that you accept Visa/MasterCard, Discover, or American Express through your own terminal.

Ship-to Locations

There are two main options when specifying your shipping terms: will ship, and will not ship. If you are interested in only selling to local buyers, then you should choose "will not ship." For all other sellers, you must choose "will ship" and then select the countries to which you're willing to ship.

Shipping internationally can be risky as much of the fraud that occurs on eBay is perpetrated by people outside the United States—as in the famous "Nigeria" scam. Some PowerSellers refuse to ship any items outside the United States to reduce risk of falling victim to scams. Other PowerSellers have no qualms with shipping worldwide. Decide for yourself which best suits you and your business. If you do decide to ship internationally, be extra cautious. Make sure that your payment clears, that the address is legitimate, and that all the proper customs forms are filled out accurately.

Shipping and Sales Tax

There are three main options when setting your shipping preferences: flat fee, calculated fees, and freight.

Flat

If you would like to designate a flat shipping rate for all your items to all locations, you can do so in the first shipping tab. You can select up to three different carriers and specify the fees you will charge for each.

Calculated

To more closely estimate what the shipping charges will be for individual bidders, you can choose to use a calculated rate. To do so, you must enter the item's shipping weight and dimensions, and then select up to three carriers. Upon winning an auction, the buyer will insert his or her zip code and the fees will be calculated accordingly. If you are looking to make shipping and handling a profit source, this method will not work for you.

Freight

For large items that weigh more than 150 pounds, eBay offers freight shipping options. Anyone selling auto parts probably won't need freight shipping—unless they're shipping pallets of car frames. If you find that you do need freight shipping, simply follow the steps on the freight tab and your auction will be marked accordingly.

Sales Tax

If your state requires you to charge sales tax on internet purchases, you will need to select your state from the pull-down menu and enter the tax rate in the text field. You can leave this section blank if your state does not require you to charge tax.

Return Policy

If you plan to accept returns on items, you will need to check the "Returns Accepted" box and then fill in the terms under which you will accept returns.

Payment Instructions

Use this field to state any special payment instructions for your bidders. Even if you do not require special payment arrangements, it is a good idea to reiterate your payment policies here. You can never be too clear when dealing with your buyers.

Review and Submit

Now that you have configured your auction as you would like, you may review all the decisions you've made and edit anything that needs fixing. Double check every piece of your auction for accuracy. Spell check your title, description, and shipping and payment policies. It is important that you present everything professionally.

Your auction listing fees will be displayed at the bottom of this page. If everything looks in order, click "submit" and begin your auction. If you have not chosen to schedule your auction, it will begin immediately and end after the duration you've chosen expires.

Congratulations—you've submitted your first auction on eBay! Now you get to sit back and watch the bidders bid. Good luck!

eBay Stores

Along with putting merchandise up for auction on eBay, you may want to consider opening an eBay Store, which would allow you to sell your fixed price and auction items from a unique destination on eBay. eBay Stores make it easy to cross-sell your inventory and build repeat business.

According to eBay, you should open an eBay Store if you want the following: to have all your listings displayed in one customizable place; to be able to easily generate repeat business and encourage multiple purchases from the same buyers; to control what you cross-sell to your customers; to maintain a larger permanent inventory than you can sell through auctions.

eBay Stores offer a convenient selling platform for all your eBay listings—auctions, fixed price items, and store inventory. eBay promotes stores in several ways. All your auction listings will contain the eBay Store icon; when bidders click on that icon, they will be taken to your store. That icon is also attached to your eBay user ID for increased visibility. The eBay Store directory is designed to promote all stores and will drive buyers to your particular store. You will also receive your own personalized eBay Store web site address that you can distribute and publicize as you wish.

The process of opening an eBay Store is almost as simple as setting up your initial user ID. The only requirements are that you be a registered eBay seller and have a minimum feedback rating of 20 or be ID-verified.

Any items that you have in active listings at the time you open your store will not appear in your store. But any auctions or fixed priced listings you post once your store is opened will automatically appear in your eBay Store.

The cost of a basic eBay Store is a nominal monthly fee (current rates can be found on www.ebay.com) that increases with the level of services you desire, along with additional fees for items listed and sold. Store inventory listings are less expensive than auction listings and appear for a longer time. Those listings appear only in your store, however, and do not come up in traditional eBay auction searches.

In addition to insertion fees, as with auctions, you also pay final-value fees when an item in a store listing sells.

eBay offers three store levels: basic, featured, and anchor. All have their own customizable storefront and the ability to list store inventory, but featured and anchor stores include additional services. Here's how the three levels differ from one another:

1. *Basic*. Your store is automatically listed in the eBay Stores Directory and will appear in every category directory where you have items listed.
2. *Featured*. Your store rotates through a special featured section on the eBay Stores home page; receives priority placement in "related stores" on search and listings pages; and it is featured within the category directory pages where you have items listed. In addition, you receive monthly reports on your sales and marketplace performance.
3. *Anchor*. In addition to the services offered to featured stores, your store

> "We have been on eBay for many years, though we just opened our store a few years ago. It is a more economical way to list your items, especially if you have a lot of merchandise to sell."
>
> —swedeng

can be showcased with your logo within the eBay Stores Directory pages. It will also receive premium placement in "related stores" on search and listings pages, which means your store will be placed higher on the page than the featured stores.

Check the eBay web site for current store subscription fees.

Setting Up Your Store

You want to apply the same principles to stocking your eBay Store that you would to a brick-and-mortar store. eBay allows you to create up to 300 custom categories and subcategories for your products, similar to aisles in a physical store.

You may decide to use product-based categories or you might use a more flexible system, with categories such as "sale items," "bestsellers," and "seasonal." Consider having a category for new items so people who visit your store regularly can quickly see what you've added recently. These custom categories can be changed and updated as often as you wish, which is a significant benefit to a seller whose inventory changes frequently.

> "I sell more out of my store—probably 60 to 70 percent of my sales. The rest sell from auctions."
>
> —truckpartsaz

Your store site should also clearly explain how you operate. Take advantage of the "Store Policies" page to provide a complete and professional description of your policies and procedures. Use "About My Store" to establish your credentials and provide some history about you and your company. Make sure that each store listing incorporates the same features as a traditional auction with a good title, clear pictures, and adequate description.

> **EBAY TIP**
>
> Use your store to list all the items you have in your inventory that complement your active auctions, and mention your store in all your eBay listings.

Use Your Store to Cross-Sell and Up-Sell

All eBay Store subscriptions have the advantage of strategically placing promotion boxes in storefronts on different pages that can highlight featured items, provide special announcements, or be used in a variety of ways to showcase your store.

You also get cross-promotion tools that help you up-sell by allowing you to control which items your buyers see after they bid on or buy one of your items, or use the checkout function after a transaction has ended. You can choose different items to show on each listing.

The tools work by allowing you to establish "merchandising relationships" for the items you list; this determines which items the buyers will be shown. You determine what goes together by designating relationships for as many or as few items as you'd like. If you don't include cross-merchandise on one of your items, eBay will automatically select related items you are selling to display to your buyers.

> "The majority of our items, probably 95 percent, are sold through auctions. Though, in the winter months, we move almost everything over to our store. However, since the bulk of our sales are in the summer, we still end up with greater sales overall through auctions."
>
> —techchoiceparts

Understand the Commitment

Your eBay Store is open for business 24/7, whether you're awake or asleep. You need to monitor your store closely, answer questions from shoppers promptly, ship merchandise on schedule and as promised, and deal with any other customer service issues that might arise as soon as possible.

If you go on vacation or are going to be away from your store for any reason, you can either arrange for someone else to monitor the site and take care of your business or place your store "on vacation" with eBay for an indefinite period. You will continue to be charged the normal store subscription and listing fees, however.

CHAPTER 6

Pricing

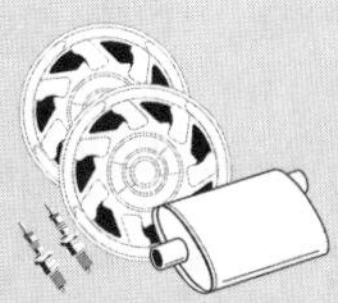

Pricing is a contentious issue among eBay PowerSellers. Some swear by setting a low starting price and a high reserve price, while others avoid reserve prices outright fearing that they sabotage the auction's final sale price and result in lower profits per item. There is no right answer, and the method that will work best for you depends largely on the nature of your target bidders, the popularity of your auctions, and the retail price of your items.

This chapter will provide you with an introduction to all the different prices you'll need to set when creating an auction, and the strategies used by PowerSellers when setting those prices. You will need to tinker with these different strategies to find the ones that produce the highest profits for you.

Starting Price

An auction's starting price is the lowest amount that the first bidder will need to bid in order to participate in the auction. Many sellers make the case that this starting price should be set to the lowest amount that you're willing to accept for an item while retaining an acceptable profit margin. If your aim is to make a 20 percent profit on everything you sell, then this price should simply be set to 20 percent higher than what it cost you to buy, pack, and ship the item. This method is most like traditional brick-and-mortar pricing methods because it guarantees profitability. Like traditional brick-and-mortar pricing methods, however, it does not guarantee sales.

The next pricing methods are more suited to eBay's dynamic and fluid pricing phenomena. Sellers who are willing to gamble their profit margin are more likely to capitalize on the eBay buyer bidding frenzy phenomenon. The aim of this strategy is to create a frenzy around every auction by capitalizing on a bidder's competitive drive to win. This frenzy, when created successfully, drives up the item's final sale price and awards higher profits to the seller. How does one create this frenzy? There are a few ways to do it.

One Dollar, Low Reserve

First is the "One Dollar, Low Reserve," or "$1LR," method. This strategy begins by setting a $1, or lower starting price on an item. The item could be either an old tire, or a vintage Porche 911—the real-world value is not taken into account. The low starting price encourages bargain-hunting bidders to jump into the auction early. The increased number of bidders sends the item's price skyward during the auction, whittling out the less enthusiastic bidders as the price goes up. But many of the original bidders will remain, either because they know the $1LR tactic and have expected to pay a fair price for the item from the beginning, or because they are now emotionally invested in the auction and feel compelled to win. Each bid, whether by calculation or compulsion, drives up your item's price.

Listing expensive inventory for $1 would frighten any reasonable businessperson. Therefore, this method includes a safety net in the low reserve price set at the auction's outset. You should set this reserve price low enough that bidders do not become discouraged when their bids repeatedly do not surpass the hidden reserve price, yet high enough that you don't lose all your profits when the item sells. One of the keys to making this strategy work is that you must advertise that you have

> "Success with $1NR depends on a few things. How much have you invested in the item? How popular will the item be? Using a higher starting price will cost you more in listing fees and turns some people away, but then you are sure to get your profits. Listing fees are cheaper if you start at $1, but the problem is that you might end up selling for $1. It's kind of like playing the slots."
>
> —swedeng

set a low reserve somewhere in your auction. Every bidder will see that you have set a reserve price, but the amount of that reserve will be hidden from them. Reserve prices tend to scare off bidders who are skeptical that sellers are overvaluing their items, and making the reserve prices too near retail prices. Therefore, for this strategy to work, you must set the price low, and advertise that you have done so.

One Dollar, No Reserve

The most controversial pricing method is known as the "$1NR" method, or, as you may have guessed, the "One Dollar, No Reserve" method. This is similar to the $1LR strategy, though it is far riskier in that without setting a reserve price, your vintage Porche might very well sell for a dollar, leaving you with the financial kick-in-the-teeth. Many sellers use this strategy successfully, trusting that if they have promoted the item well enough, the eBay bidding community will determine the fair market value. And because the hope of buying a valuable item for only a few dollars draws in a large number of early bidders, there is a greater chance of a bidding war developing and driving profits through the roof.

> "I don't think $1NR helps the final price. I think people are leaning more toward instant gratification. We do $1NR auctions on either very high, or very low, demand items—or on unique inventory that people can't buy at any retailer."
>
> —sumofallparts

> "We don't do $1NR. I normally list each item at as fair a price as I can set. I do set a Buy It Now price, usually about $15 more than the starting price, so if someone needs the item fast, they have that option. I do not like hidden reserve auctions; it just seems unfair to the bidder to me."
>
> —techchoiceparts

Be cautious when using or experimenting with the $1NR strategy. It often falls victim to sniping, wherein savvy bidders wait until the closing seconds of an auction to place a bid, thereby not allowing time for the item's price to reach fair market value and securing a huge bargain. This method also should not be used alone, as it can prevent the growth of a business by limiting the number of similar items that can be sold at one time—the higher number of items available will lower the demand for that item, and therefore your final selling price. The $1NR method is best used as a promotional tool to draw bidders into auctions, where sellers are cross-promoting their auctions that use not-so-risky pricing strategies.

It should be noted that if you choose to use either the $1LR or $1NR method of pricing, setting your starting price at 99 cents instead of $1 would work just as effectively in drawing in bidders, but would also save you money in listing fees due to eBay's listing fee structure.

Buy It Now (BIN)

The Buy It Now price caters to convenience buyers who would rather pay your asking price than wait a week for your auction to end. More than 25 percent of the items sold on eBay are sold through stores, BIN, or other fixed-price sales. So to pass over setting a BIN price is to pass over a substantial number of your buyers. It should be used as an important part of your overall pricing strategy.

The first BIN method applies if you have opted for a conservative pricing strategy and set your starting prices at a level that would produce a profit. By setting your BIN price slightly higher than your starting price, you can encourage bidders to bypass the lengthy bidding process and purchase the item immediately. It may be worth the few extra dollars to them to skip the days of watching and bidding. This method works well with relatively inexpensive items that are not likely to create a bidding frenzy, or with items that are in high demand where you are confident that you will receive your asking price.

The second BIN method is used in conjunction with the $1NR promotional strategy. By setting a BIN price within a $1NR auction, you are achieving two things: attracting a high number of potential convenience buyers, and planting a suggestion in the minds of the bidders as to what is a fair price for the item at auction. eBay buyers are smart and often do research, both on eBay

> "I have never used $1NR. I can't risk selling for less than my cost, but I don't have any problems with the strategy. I think it can be really useful for smaller items."
>
> —truckpartsaz

and off, to find the fair market value for the item you are selling. But that doesn't mean that setting a BIN price for them to bid toward will not affect bidding habits.

Reserve Price

There is little strategy behind setting a reserve price. Bidders tend to opt for auctions without a set reserve price due to the promise of a better bargain, and therefore this price should be used sparingly. Though if you are testing a new item to see what kind of bids it produces, or cannot bear to see it sell for less than a certain amount, then a reserve price is a good idea. PowerSellers rarely use reserves, and in some cases, when they do opt to use a reserve price, they go so far as to state what the reserve price is in the item's description. This provides the seller with a price guarantee, and the bidder with the knowledge of how much they would need to pony up.

Setting, and advertising, a reserve price, in essence, negates the usual function of the starting price. It makes the starting price obsolete, allowing the seller to post an item for $1 or less to attract more initial viewers to the auction, while maintaining their usual starting price safety net in the advertised reserve price. It's a clever strategy. Unfortunately, there's no data to show whether it is effective in drawing in more bidders.

Profitability vs. Risk

Finding an effective pricing strategy is an exercise in balancing profitability and risk. A high-risk strategy may yield a few highly profitable sales, but it will not do so reliably. A conservative strategy can guarantee that every sale you make is reliably profitable, but sales could be slow or yield small profits.

The most effective pricing plan makes use of a combination of these strategies. High-risk strategies are effective in attracting the attention of bidders. Use cross-promotion within those high-risk auctions as promotional tools for your low-risk auctions, fixed-price items, and store. Soon, your high-risk auctions will be leading bidders into your other, more reliably profitable sales channels within eBay.

CHAPTER 7

Selling **Your Items**

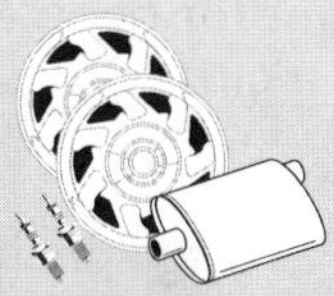

Now that you're familiar with the logistics of starting an auction on eBay, it is time for some fine tuning. To receive the highest price for your items, you will need to put some thought and care into your auction. There are three main areas: the title, the description, and the photos.

The importance of creating quality titles, descriptions, and photos in your auctions cannot be understated. This is your opportunity to communicate directly to buyers. With the competition as fierce as it is in the Parts & Accessories category, you must communicate effectively.

The Title

The auction title has two important jobs. First and foremost it provides the keywords that eBay uses to produce results when buyers use the site's search function. Most buyers find their items through eBay's search function, and while it is possible for buyers to search both title and description, the site's default setting searches only auction titles. So be sure when writing your title to use any keywords that a buyer might choose when searching for your item. Remember, the title has a limit of 55 characters.

Second, the title displays information about the items on which anyone browsing the auction can bid. Therefore it is important that your title be more than just a collection of keywords for the search engine; it must be legible to bidders in order for people to visit your auction.

Here are some things to keep in mind when writing your titles.

Always include, if available:

- Manufacturer's name
- Model number
- Series name
- Item condition
- From/for what model vehicle
- Pertinent information (color, size, complete set, etc.)

Avoid:

- Space-wasting attention grabbers (L@@K!!)
- ALL CAPS

- Unconventional abbreviations
- Adjectives (use these in your description)

Here are two titles for the same set of mud flaps.

Good Title

Yosemite Sam Mud Flaps Black Fits all GMC trucks NIB

Bad Title

AWESOME!!! Loony Toons Mud Flaps W@W GR8!

The first title is packed with information to help the buyer know exactly what is up for auction. It contains keywords that a buyer would use to search for such a set of mud flaps, and all of the abbreviations used are industry standards that buyers seeking this item would know. "NIB" means "new in box" and is an eBay standard abbreviation. The second title may catch the bidder's eye more readily than the other titles on the page, but it contains few keywords, or usable information. It misspells the brand name, and wastes space with exclamation points, useless adjectives, and visual tricks. Not only would this second title not come up in searches, but it gives the bidder little indication of what they will see if they look at this auction. The bidder would not waste time with this listing and would move on.

Description

Investing time in writing a good description will pay off in the price you receive. Your description should include the following:

- The name of the item
- What the item is made of
- When and where the item was made
- Who made the item (company, manufacturer, etc.)
- What condition the item is in
- Weight, size, and/or dimensions of the item
- Notable features or markings on the item
- Any special background or history

Everything in your description must be true and accurate. If an item is damaged or missing parts, do not say something vague, such as "easily restored." If possible, identify exactly what needs to be replaced or suggest the buyer purchase the item to be used as parts for another piece. You might also add a personal touch to your description; many sellers have found that doing so can increase bids and sales. For example, say what the item is for, how it can help the buyer, and what prerequisites exist for a buyer to use the item, such as owning the appropriate model car. If the item is not in perfect condition, be honest. Describe any scratches, chips, stains, and other imperfections.

Avoid something known as keyword spamming—including words in your description that are not actually related to your item just because they are words a search would pick up. This is against eBay's listing policies. Do use as many legitimate search words and phrases in your description as possible, however, to be sure your item will come up when bidders search.

You can also use your description to add details about shipping costs, payment terms, and any other details you think may be of interest to a bidder.

> "I don't spend a whole lot of time interacting directly with customers. I try to include as much detail in my listing as I can, so most of the e-mailing I do is about shipping or sending tracking information to buyers."
>
> —truckpartsaz

Even if you plan to charge your customers the precise shipping cost, it's always a good idea to include at least an estimate of what the shipping cost will be so bidders aren't surprised when the auction is over. Also, let bidders know if there are any restrictions on where you will ship, such as United States only, United States and Canada only, or certain international locations. eBay has a shipping calculator that you can insert in your auctions that allows the buyer to determine how much it will cost to send that specific item to their address via USPS or UPS.

When you're finished, proofread, spell check, and proofread again.

Pictures Worth More than 1,000 Words

A photo, indicated by a camera icon or a thumbnail image of your item in the auction list, will make a tremendous difference in the success of your auction. Quality photos not only let bidders see what your product really looks like, but they also say that you're a serious, professional eBay seller.

> "For auctions, we normally take a photo of the exact item we're selling. If it's an item that we stock, and the item will always look the same, we usually just relist the same item with the same photo. We use a Sony FD Mavica digital camera, with 3.5 floppy disk. It's a very convenient camera to use. When we purchased new computers, I actually bought external floppy drives so we wouldn't have to get another camera."
>
> —techchoiceparts

Create a photo area in your home or shop with good lighting and a backdrop for an uncluttered background. Consider developing a photo backdrop with a distinctive color, pattern, logo, or company name that helps brand your business. If appropriate, showcase your item with accessories to display it to its best advantage. Be sure to indicate whether or not those accessories are included in the auction, are available separately, or are not for sale. A box draped with a piece of plain fabric works as a display pedestal. Maintain a database of pictures so it's easy to pull up images for listings when you are selling items you've sold before.

Invest in a digital camera. You don't have to get the top-of-the-line, but get a camera that has more than two megapixels and a macro function for clear close-up shots. Your customers will want to see the intricacies of stitching in leather, welds along seems, texture of material, etc. Therefore, a macro function for clarity up close is important.

If you have a scanner, you can use print film and then scan your photos. This process is time-consuming and costly, however. If you plan to sell on eBay with any regularity, invest in a digital camera.

Once you have the pictures uploaded to your computer, you can then use a program to adjust and enhance your images. Be sure that all the parts of the image are bright and clear.

> "I have a 5.3MP HP Photosmart. The pixels are great—which is important. I take my pictures and edit them in Photoshop to change the background and size. Soon I will be watermarking them as well. Then, I save them and name them under their Volvo part number. That way I can easily select them for the listing when I make it."
>
> —swedeng

Copyrights

When writing your descriptions and uploading your photos, be sure that you are using original content. The practice of cutting and pasting item descriptions from a manufacturer's web site is common because it makes quick work of providing accurate information. This practice can be dangerous, however, as some manufacturers copyright the promotional materials for their products. If you choose to use text or photos from an outside source in your auction listings, be sure that it is not copyrighted material. The lack of a copyright symbol does not mean that it is free to use. Contact the company and ask for permission to use their photos or text; most manufacturers are happy to give such permission. Though it only takes one disgruntled corporate lawyer to ruin your day. When in doubt, it is best to create original content.

CHAPTER 8

Customer **Care**

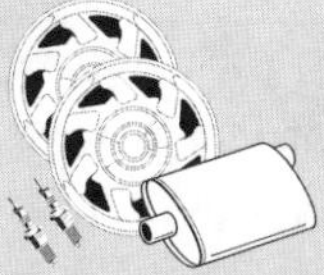

Even before you submit your auction to eBay, you must be thinking about customer care. eBay bidders are sophisticated people, and care every bit as much about the way they are treated as real-world retail shoppers do. This proper treatment begins when you are putting together your item's auction page.

Bidders expect your auction page to be professional, attractive, error-free, and easy to use. If your page has typos, incorrect information, fuzzy photos, or just plain-old hard to read bricks of text, bidders will shop somewhere else. Take extra care to consider your bidders when formatting and writing your auction pages. Be sure to

> "We use a combination of tools to make sure we supply the correct part. We have an AAIA (Automotive Aftermarket Industry Association) database of every vehicle on the road. Integrated into that are OE part numbers for every A/C compressor built. We also use several methods of reseaerch to back up that data, including Mitchell, AllData, and our competitors' catalogs. Sometimes, we will actually seek out a specific vehicle to find or confirm the exact parts that are on it."
>
> —techchoiceparts

invite bidders to contact you with questions. In addition to eBay's "Ask Seller a Question" link, provide an e-mail address and a phone number where you can be reached. Make it as easy as possible for bidders to do business with you as you can.

When writing your description, try to anticipate questions bidders might ask you. Answer any hypothetical questions you can think of. Taking some extra time when writing your descriptions could save you hours spent answering e-mails and phone calls.

During Auctions

During auctions you will need to be available to your customers in case a few of them need to ask you questions. As any PowerSeller will tell you, answering questions from bidders will quickly become a lot of work.

Skype

In September 2005, eBay purchased the online communications company Skype, which produces the Voice over Internet

Protocol (VoIP) program of the same name. Skype is a free download that installs on Windows, Linux, Mac OS X, and Pocket PC systems. The company has more than 113 million registered users in over 225 countries around the globe. The program enables users to make free voice "telephone" calls from their computers to anyone in the world who is also running Skype. For a low per minute rate, Skype users can also send and receive calls to and from regular telephone numbers.

> "I try to list the applications for the product in the description. Though, I do have a little disclaimer on there due to the many different notes and circumstances that exist with chassis splits etc. I offer that people can e-mail me their year, model, and VIN number so that I can verify that the item will work for them."
>
> —swedeng

Clear communication is at the heart of every successful eBay sale. eBay exists because of its ability to bring together buyers and sellers from all over the world. By integrating Skype into its services, eBay will provide sellers with the ability to offer free voice communication during a sale whether the buyer is in Boston or Boca Raton.

One of the drawbacks to Skype is that sending clear audio back and forth simultaneously over an internet connection is bandwidth heavy. In order for the program to work well enough for people to have an actual conversation, each user must have a high-speed broadband connection. If you are stuck on a dial-up, satellite, or slower connection, Skype will not work for you. If you enjoy the speed of a cable connection or something even faster, however, downloading and integrating Skype into your auctions, store listings, and "contact us" information will be well worth your time.

To integrate Skype into your eBay world, you will need to first download the program at www.skype.com. It is a surprisingly lightweight download and will take not more than a few minutes to download and install. Open the program and click "Create a New Account" on the opening screen.

Once you have registered, your contact list will open. This contact list format will be familiar to anyone who has used any variation of an instant messaging program. You have the ability to contact anyone on your contact list via instant messaging or voice call. If you know someone who already uses Skype, or have telephone numbers you'd like to call through Skype, you can add them to your contact list through the "Contacts" menu.

Now, to let all your eBay customers know that you are offering Skype calls for your business, you'll have to put notice on your auctions and listings. Instead of simply placing some text inviting your customers to contact you via Skype (as is necessary with telephone numbers and e-mail addresses), you have the ability to create a button on your pages that allows fellow Skype users to initiate a call to you with a single click. To create this button, proceed to the Account menu and select "Go to My Account Page." Once you have logged into your My Account page on the Skype web site, click "Share" in the top menu. Down the page a bit you'll see an option for "Create a Skype Button." Click this to proceed.

Enter your new Skype name in box 1, select a button style in box 2, preview your button in box 3, and copy the code for your button in box 4. Paste this snippet of code into your eBay auction, listings, and contact information boxes. This will place the Skype button on your eBay pages, and customers who are inclined to call you with questions can now do so for free.

This button will automatically show your customers when you are online and available to take calls, and when you're away. Skype also gives you the option of forwarding all your Skype calls to a traditional telephone number so that you can receive sales calls on your home phone, mobile phone, or anywhere else.

Skype is an extremely useful tool that is catching on fast. It is popular in Europe where both high-speed internet connections and high-priced international telephone rates are ubiquitous. eBay's purchase of Skype will only add to its popularity and it will soon be as common as mobile phones, instant messengers, and e-mail.

Integrating Skype into your eBay sales will help your buyers get their questions answered. It will help you build your buyers' confidence, expand your geographic market, and help you close sales.

Questions

Answering questions from bidders can become a tiresome and frustrating task. There will be nights when you are tired, it is

> "Nearly all of my time is spent interacting with the customer, either directly on the phone or via e-mail. Purchasing high-dollar items over the internet is still a little worrisome to the majority of consumers, so much of our time is spent taking the time to talk to our customers. By letting them get to know us a little bit, they are more comfortable spending money with us."
>
> —techchoiceparts

2 A.M., and you've got 50 more questions to answer. It is during these times that you must keep your feedback score in mind. Be polite and professional in your answers. If you are receiving the same question over and over again, write a polite and thorough answer once and then cut and paste it to the 20 people who need it. Any question that comes to you through the eBay message center will be posted on the auction's page for future questioners to see. The more patient you are with your customers, the more loyal they will be to you in the future.

There will come a point when you will need to hire someone to help you slog through all the questions. When selling specialty items, such as parts for classic cars, you will receive more questions than most sellers. People don't bother so much about specifics when buying textbooks or old monitors off eBay. When it comes to restoring classics, however, bidders will need to know every last detail about your product. Make sure the person you hire to help you answer questions is as knowledgeable about your products are you are.

Post Auction

Once an auction ends, be sure to contact the winner right away to congratulate him or her and present the next steps. Constant and clear communication will help the transaction occur smoothly. As soon after the end of the auction as you can, send an invoice with the item number, the auction's total price, and instructions for submitting payment to you. Be sure to thank the winner for his or her business and give the e-mail a personal tone. For a nominal fee eBay will automate this for you. Many PowerSellers take advantage of this option, but caution new sellers to make sure the e-mail does not sound automated. Customers would rather deal with a person than a machine, even though sometimes it just isn't feasible for sellers.

> "With motorcycles, there are so many variations on parts that it is a full-time job just finding out what our customers need. Then, it's a full-time job supporting them. We calculate about an hour, per customer, per transaction for each item we sell. It's very time consuming to get them the right stuff."
>
> —sumofallparts

After the winning bidder has submitted payment, they will expect a receipt and quick shipment of their item. Many PowerSellers, when they do receive negative feedback, get it because the bidder was disappointed with the speed of shipping. Be sure to contact the buyer if you cannot ship an item immediately. If you know about a possible delay prior to posting an auction, mention it

> "I have had one or two problems with fraud, mostly using someone else's username or PayPal account. Despite that, I have had no losses; they were both caught by PayPal before I shipped."
>
> —truckpartsaz

in the auction's description. It is better to be honest than to disappoint people.

Once the payment has been received and the package has been shipped, e-mail the bidder to let him know that his item is on the way. If you have shipped via a carrier that uses a tracking number, include that in the e-mail so that the bidder can know when the item will arrive.

Then, once the transaction is complete, provide timely positive feedback if it is warranted. If you've done everything right, you will be rewarded with positive feedback in return. Remember, you cannot make everyone happy. Though as evidenced by the overwhelmingly positive feedback ratings of some PowerSellers, it is possible to come pretty darn close.

When Things Go Wrong

Sometimes you will make mistakes. For the most part, buyers are understanding people and will be forgiving if you are straightforward with them. When mistakes happen, do what you need to do to make things right for the customer. Remember, this is your business; you have the power and authority to do what needs to be done. Don't hesitate to offer a partial or full refund if it means keeping a customer.

If you run into a belligerent customer who cannot be reasoned with, remain calm. You may receive quite unpleasant e-mails or worse from angry customers, but you must not allow it to affect how you deal with the problem. Read the customer's entire e-mail, apologize for the problem, ask how you can best solve the dilemma, and then thank him or her for their patience and understanding . . . even if they showed you none. You will be surprised how many irate customers can be turned into grateful customers with a polite and apologetic e-mail.

> "We do see some fraud. More often, it's attempted fraud. We're pretty good at spotting the phishing e-mails, or the people who want to send a money order for an amount that is way over the sales price, and ask us to send the remainder back to them. I think we've only been burned twice. Also, I probably get 10 to 15 e-mails per day alleging to be from PayPal or eBay claiming either that my account has been compromised, and I need to click a link to verify it; or that I've been upgraded to a new program and I just need to click a link to sign up. Luckily those e-mails are pretty easy to weed out."
>
> —techchoiceparts

Beware of Scams

One of the most well-known scams on eBay occurs when a winning bidder receives an item from the seller and immediately contacts the seller with a complaint of some sort. Most times the buyer will complain of damage during shipping, or the misstated condition of the item, or an incorrect shipment.

> "The fraud we see is mostly illegal charge-backs. We lack the resources to fight them and people know they can hurt us by just starting a claim. We document everything, but even so, if it's just a $50 charge-back we can't allocate three hours to fighting with the credit card company. Using PayPal really hedges a lot of the risk for us, too."
>
> —sumofallparts

The buyer will then demand a full or partial refund and threaten to post negative feedback if the seller does not comply. As a seller, it would seem that you have two poor options: comply or take the negative feedback. But that is not the case. If you deem the item worth the cost of attempting recovery, you have a third option. In a pleasant and understanding tone, apologize for the damage/mistake and offer either an exchange if you have an identical item in stock, or a full refund upon receipt of the damaged or incorrect item. In this scenario you may need to cough up the return shipping charges, but at least you're not losing the value of the item or being scammed out of honestly earned revenue.

Conflict Resolution

eBay will rarely provide aid in a conflict between a buyer and seller. In most cases you are on your own to settle conflicts professionally. eBay will come to your aid in certain circumstances, however. Here are a few:

- eBay receives a court order finding that feedback you've received is slanderous or illegal in some way.

- Feedback you've received has obscene, racist, or vulgar language.
- Feedback you've received reveals your personal information, such as your home address.
- A buyer has bid on your items for the sole purpose of leaving negative feedback.

In these instances you are encouraged to contact eBay for help. In most other instances, you're left to your own devices.

> "We've been blessed with a couple of really good account managers at eBay, both named Todd. There have been a couple of times when I really need a quick answer to something, and either one of them would get back to us just about right away, either by e-mail or phone. Other than that, it's been all live and learn."
>
> —techchoiceparts

Don't Fight Fire with Fire

Sellers have the ability to respond to negative feedback that they feel is unwarranted. If you choose to respond to negative feedback you have received—and you should—don't use it as a way to fight back. Remain calm and stick to the facts. For example, if you get burned with negative feedback for late shipping, but you stated clearly in your auction that shipping would be delayed for this item, simply make a note of that underneath the negative feedback. For example:

Negative: *Seller waited five days before shipping out my oil filters!*

Reply: *Delayed ship date was clearly stated in item description for duration of auction.*

Try to remain calm, factual, and emotionless. The potential bidders who read your feedback comments will appreciate your cool-headed professionalism.

CHAPTER 9

Starting a Business

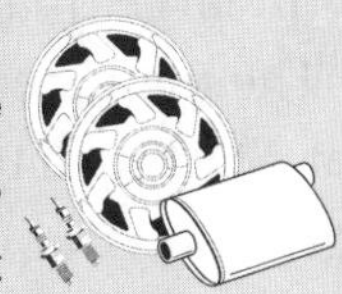

Starting any business, whether it is based on eBay or not, requires careful planning. Before you invest the family savings in thousands of gas tank caps or cow-print seat covers, you should sit down and think through your upcoming adventure. There are many things to consider. In this chapter, we'll cover the most important ones, and then provide you with some places to find help when you need it.

Finances

There are two ways to go about building your business financially. You can start small, using some extra personal funds to buy inventory, and then slowly build your inventory and subsequent sales as you begin collecting profits. Or you can seek out a bank loan to help you stock your shelves and begin your business with more sales and faster turnover.

Building your business slowly is the safer option financially because of the low start-up costs. It does require time, patience, and a lot of work in addition to your day job, however. This method also gives your larger competition the ability to beat you on price. When you are first starting out, you'll need to buy from your item sources in small quantities, which is often more expensive per item than buying in large quantities. Larger sellers who are able to buy large quantities for the discounts are then able to offer their items at lower prices. Their higher sales volume also produces more revenue (and profits) for them per month, making it even easier for them to buy in large quantities.

The main benefit to starting slowly is that you'll be free of debt. Starting a business without a loan gives you the freedom to grow at your own pace, take time off if necessary, and even pull the plug if you decide that selling on eBay isn't for you.

Taking out a loan could make your start-up easier. You will be able to buy inventory in larger quantities, sell more items, and sell for lower prices, making competing with other sellers easier right off the bat. Getting the loan itself will be challenging, however. Banks do not pass out money to start-ups. In fact, most banks will not provide your business with a loan unless you have already established reliable item sources, a solid customer base, and a track record of profits that proves your business's ability to make payments on the loan. These requirements sometimes make it hard for start-ups to find financing. But there are options.

> "When we first started our business, we borrowed about $40,000. I and the other owner kicked in about $50,000 each to get started, and away we went."
>
> —techchoiceparts

If you feel confident in your business, you might consider taking out a personal loan or a second mortgage on your home. This is considerably more risky than a business loan because if your business fails you stand to lose your house and income in one blow. Also, because it is a personal loan, you will still owe the bank long after the business is gone. So if you decide to take this route, be sure that you have done all the planning and anticipation that you can, right down to the smallest detail.

Business Type

For tax purposes you will need to define your business to the IRS. There are several types of business classifications to choose from, each with benefits and drawbacks. Choose the one that best suits your intentions.

Sole Proprietorship

A sole proprietorship is the most common type of start-up business because it requires little paperwork. You are the only owner. Legally, financially, and tax-wise there is no difference between you and your business. Your business's assets are your assets. Your business's debt is your personal debt. And your business's profits are your income.

The advantage to this type of business is that it is easy to start and you keep all the profits. You need only to file a business income form (Schedule C) along with your regular taxes. The disadvantage of this type of business is that you are personally liable for all the business debt—and mistakes. If your business is sued for any reason, you are directly sued.

Partnership

A partnership is similar to a sole proprietorship, except that instead of one proprietor, there are two. Both parties are legally and financially responsible for the business. Some partnerships are based on common interests (such as husband-wife teams), and some are based on financial need (such as the financier and the manager).

If you're interested in setting up a partnership, be sure to be excruciatingly clear going into the business about who takes on what role, who makes what decisions, and who receives what money. A clearly defined relationship will go a long way toward making the business partnership a success.

Corporation

Unlike a sole proprietorship or partnership, a corporation is its own legal entity. A corporation's debt, taxes, profits, and legal liability are separate from the corporate owner. While this provides immense protection for owners, corporations can be tricky and expensive to get started, and are therefore not often the first choice of start-up businesses. If you're interested in starting a corporation, you should contact an attorney in your area for help.

S Corporations

An S corporation provides tax benefits to owners. Instead of being taxed twice as a corporation is—once as corporate income tax and once on owner dividends—an S corporation doesn't pay taxes on its corporate income. Owners only pay taxes on their own income from the S corporation.

S corporations also offer all the same legal and financial protections that corporations do, so this may be a smarter choice for your start-up.

Limited Liability Corporation

Like an S corporation, limited liability corporations (LLCs) provide owners with legal and financial protection, while avoiding the double taxation that occurs in corporations. This is quickly becoming the default choice for small businesses. Setting up an LLC is relatively easy as well. Talk to your local chamber of commerce or Service Corp of Retired Executives (SCORE) chapter about where to find the necessary forms.

Registering Your Business Name

In many states it is necessary for you to register your business name, sometimes called a "fictitious name," before you can do such things as open a business bank account or apply for a bank

> "Inventory management is the bane of most companies' existence. I'm an old Microsoft Excel guy, so I prefer to have everything inventoried in an Excel database. Doing it this way, I can filter, look up, or massage the data however I choose."
>
> —techchoiceparts

loan. Registering your business name also ensures that you have the rights to that name in your state. Other companies will still be able to operate under your registered name, but if it ever came to a legal battle, you would have claim. Registration is a simple process that involves a short form, a small processing fee, and a stamp. Check with your state's Small Business Association web site for more information.

Inventory Issues

Buying your inventory can be seen as the "no turning back" point. Once you've made such a large investment, you're committed to making the business work. That's why it is important to take care of your inventory as closely as you would if it were the actual cash equivalent.

Storage

Your inventory must be stored safely in an appropriate facility. A lot of the items you'll be dealing in require a dry and clean storage area. Fabric items such as fuzzy dice or seat covers can collect mold and grow soggy. All metal parts will begin to rust in damp places. Cardboard boxes must be kept up off the concrete floor to prevent moisture damage. Your inventory must also be stored in a manner that makes it easy to retrieve the items you need without moving a bunch of boxes around to get to them. Continuously moving boxes of fragile equipment will, over time, destroy your inventory.

Many PowerSellers who started their businesses in their basements quickly realized that the damp, dark, soggy conditions were less than ideal for their needs. Before long these sellers were able to rent storage facilities in the less-expensive industrial areas around their towns. The low rents and large facilities suit their businesses perfectly. They have plenty of space to store their inventories, lots of room for their shipping departments, and outdoor areas big enough for the FedEx or UPS trucks to back up to the loading docks. A fancy and expensive Main Street storefront is not required as all of their selling occurs online.

Before you make the investment in inventory, be sure that you have arranged for the proper facilities to receive, manage, store, and ship that inventory.

> "We have two warehouses now, but we did initially work from our home. We didn't move into a building until we knew we could handle the overhead."
>
> —sumofallparts

Materials

Besides investing in your inventory, you will also need to make an investment in supplies for your business. You will obviously need a computer, though a computer capable of loading eBay can be found quite inexpensively these days. You will also need shipping materials that are appropriate for your items. As the seller, it is your responsibility to make sure your items are packed in such a way that they can withstand a reasonable amount of abuse while in transit.

You can find all these items on eBay. Savvy sellers have realized that one of the largest markets on eBay is, in fact, other sellers; packing and shipping materials are therefore quite easy to find at great prices. If you're in a rush and don't want to wait a few days for delivery, try your local Staples, Office Depot, UPS Store, or U-Haul supply store. They all generally have adequate packing and shipping departments.

CHAPTER 10

Helpful **Tools**

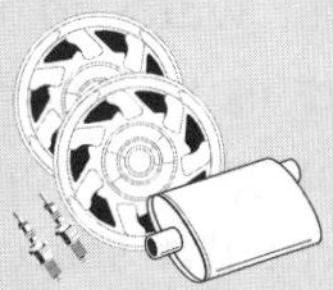

An industry is growing to aid eBay sellers. Research, software, and consulting companies are being created every day to help sellers sell. As a result, many tools are available to you to make selling easier, faster, and more cost efficient. Even eBay itself provides many tools to help you along. In this chapter, we'll cover some of eBay's own tools and some of the third-party solutions that are available to help you reach PowerSeller status.

To help sellers discover even more helpful tools, eBay has created a directory full of third-party solutions. Visit the directory by clicking the "Solutions Directory" link on the left side of eBay's main page.

Research Tools

Choosing the correct items to sell is a key factor to your business's success. To help you make an informed decision, companies have released the following research tools. Be sure to take advantage of at least one of these services before you begin selling in earnest.

eBay Pulse

eBay Pulse, at http://pulse.ebay.com, will provide you with some general information about the current popular trends in eBay buying and selling. Choose "eBay Motors" from the pull-down menu to find the latest trends in the category. This simple page will tell you the most popular eBay Motors category searches, the largest eBay Motors stores, and the most watched items. This information changes every day, and is therefore a good thing to keep an eye on. Click through the top searches to find top selling items for that particular search term. Is there anything in there that you might like to sell? Who is selling the most of these items? Can you find ways to do it better? Browse through the largest stores to find out what they've got to offer. eBay Pulse is a great place to begin thinking about what the hot items are on eBay Motors, and what you would like to begin selling. Unfortunately, eBay Pulse doesn't offer any specific Parts & Accessories information, so you'll have to go through all the popular eBay Motors searches to find the ones in your category.

Marketplace Research

eBay also offers a service called Marketplace Research. This tool provides a place for sellers to do more in-depth research about the items they are, or hope to begin, selling. Sellers can find up to 90 days of completed listing information, as opposed to the usual 30 days available through Advanced Search; top searches in a particular category or across the whole site; average sale and average start price for any given item; and lots of other information.

There are three subscription levels: Fast Pass, Basic, and Pro. Fast Pass is a nonrenewing two-day subscription for $2.99. Basic and Pro are monthly subscriptions that can be had for $9.99 and $24.99 respectively. You can view the details of Marketplace Research and the services offered for the different subscription levels at http://pages.ebay.com/marketplace_research/.

This service receives mixed reviews from sellers. Some complain that it is overpriced and limited in its services, while others applaud the service as being helpful and thorough. Visit the Marketplace Research discussion board to read some reviews before taking the plunge. In our experience it has been quite helpful for quick research, though limited in its offerings compared to the more established eBay research companies.

Terapeak.com

Terapeak.com's Marketplace Research tool is similar to eBay's Marketplace Research tool in that it allows you to research things such as market trends, item performance, and buyer habits for any given item or category. Terapeak is well regarded as an easy-to-use and effective service that has been helping eBay sellers since 2003. It is an online tool and requires no software download. The service has two subscription levels: Research Lite for $9.95 per month, or Research Complete for $16.95 per month or $169.50 per year.

Andale

Andale is the most well-known eBay market research company. It has been around almost since the inception of eBay itself. Its research tool is called, appropriately, Andale Research. It is a web-based tool, thereby avoiding the problems of operating-system-specific programs, and it is the lowest priced of all research tools at only $7.95 per month.

Andale Research can tell you much of the same information as the services above, such as item and category information. But it will also provide you with a recommendation for what time of the day and week to list your item for maximum profitability, and give you a comparison of an item's eBay selling price versus retail selling prices on Froogle, Shopping.com, and BizRate. And it will tell you which type of listing, such as auction or Buy It Now, will get you the best price for your item.

In addition to the market research tools, Andale offers a whole line of services to help the eBay seller, such as Sales Analyzer to help you get maximum profit from your existing listings, and Andale Supplier, a tool to help you find the best source for the items you sell.

HammerTap's DeepAnalysis 2

HammerTap offers quite a few services to help the eBay seller. Its market research tool, DeepAnalysis 2, is a software download. It helps sellers find out what is selling by analyzing data and providing reports about specific eBay sellers, categories, items, and keywords. It also helps sellers find out why particular items are selling. It finds the average starting price, auction length, and payment types accepted for items that are selling the most reliably. You can use this information to fine tune your own listings for better sales. DeepAnalysis 2 is a robust tool with many ways to help a seller, only a fraction of which we're able to cover here. It does, however, have some drawbacks. It is fairly expensive at $17.95 per month, and runs only on Windows—leaving out Mac and Linux users. Take advantage of the free trial, and then judge for yourself.

> "The closest I come to automation is TurboLister, which is a lifesaver. I also use PayPal, which is great because once the item sells, the buyer generally pays right away without having to go back and forth with us on e-mail first."
>
> —truckpartsaz

Auction Management Tools

Submitting every auction via eBay's web site would be clunky, time-consuming, and visually

> "I find TurboLister really helpful. It is a nice time-saver as far as getting listings relisted or putting up mass listings on a sale day."
>
> —swedeng

painful. No one could become a PowerSeller if they spent all their time listing individual auctions through eBay's web site. Therefore, to facilitate listing more than a few products per month, many companies have created software that helps sellers list, duplicate, relist, and manage their auctions. Here are a few that are commonly used by PowerSellers.

eBay's Tools

eBay provides the following tools to help sellers better manage their auctions:

- *TurboLister.* A bulk listing tool with HTML templates.
- *Selling Manager.* An online auction management tool that includes feedback templates, bulk relisting, invoicing, downloadable sales history, and bulk feedback. Best when used in conjunction with Turbo Lister.
- *Selling Manager Pro.* An online auction management tool that includes inventory management, listing statistics, bulk feedback and invoicing, automated e-mails, and more.
- *Blackthorne Basic.* A download application for PCs that helps sellers create listings, manage auctions, and manage customer correspondence.

- *Blackthorne Pro.* A download application for PCs that is a complete auction management tool. It creates listings, manages auctions, manages customer correspondence, handles bulk processing, and helps with post-auction tasks, such as invoicing.

> "We try to automate everything except the e-mails—those still need to be personalized. Besides those, we have systems in place that manage everything. It's not perfect, but it's a long way from where we started and we're always getting better. We use Mainstreet Commerce's Businessflow."
>
> —sumofallparts

Auctiva

Auctiva is a free tool that helps sellers create listings, schedule auctions, cross-market auctions, host images, manage sales, generate reports, and increase efficiency. It is an online tool. To learn more, or to sign up, visit www.auctiva.com.

ChannelAdvisor

ChannelAdvisor offers all levels of service from helping individual sellers manage their first few auctions, to helping large corporations liquidate entire companies. Its auction management software, ChannelAdvisor Pro, it is a web-based tool that offers templates for listings, image hosting, inventory management capabilities, customer correspondence, and post-auction checkout. One of the benefits of ChannelAdvisor is the many levels of service it provides. You will not outgrow its services. For more information, visit www.channeladvisor.com.

Photo Hosting Services

To become a PowerSeller you will need to display as many photos of your items as you can. Research shows that there is a direct relationship between the number of photos in an auction and the final sale price. Simply put, buyers want to see what they're buying, and the more you can show to them, the more likely they are to make the purchase. If you stick with eBay's photo services, adding more photos means adding to the listing price, and when you are listing several thousand items a month, a difference of 45 cents per item will add up fast. To avoid those per-photo fees, you can use one of the photo hosting services described below and then link to the photos in your auction descriptions with a simple HTML tag. You will be able to display as many photos for your auction as you would like at no incremental cost.

FotoTime

For only $23.95 per year, FotoTime provides enough storage for you to have thousands of photos online. It also provides thumbnail versions of each photo you upload for convenient placement into your auction pages. For more information, visit www.fototime.com.

VillagePhotos

VillagePhotos has many different photo hosting plans for you to choose from. It offers low prices and useful options such as a browser uploading tool, a photo album for easy management, and automatic thumbnails. If you plan to grow beyond eBay into other online marketplaces, you can use Village Photos to integrate with Yahoo! Auctions and Yahoo! Stores.

VillagePhotos' plans start at just $3.95 per month. For more information, visit www.villagephotos.com.

Photobucket.com

Photobucket.com is a free online photo hosting and album service. It has an online uploading tool, photo manager, a public photo album feature, and easy eBay integration. It also integrates well with web sites such as Myspace.com and blog sites.

These are just some of the tools that help sellers. If you can't find what you need here, visit eBay's Solution Directory to learn about hundreds of other programs. Also, you can visit www.auctionsoftwarereview.com for an independent source of auction management software downloads and reviews.

CHAPTER 11

Advanced Marketing **Strategies**

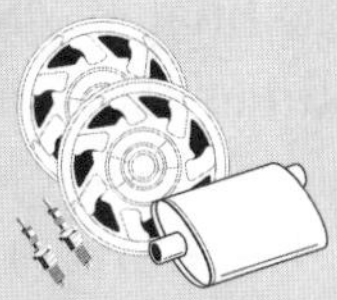

Since its launch in 1995, eBay has grown to become exactly what it touts itself to be: The World's Online Marketplace. In the early days, marketing was not much of a concern for sellers; simply listing items for auction was enough. Today, however, due to the astronomical growth in the number of auctions running at any given time, losing your auction in the crowd is a distinct possibility. And that makes marketing a must. If you are not taking steps to attract large numbers of bidders, your auction will be overshadowed. Your sales rates will suffer along with your final sale prices. Fortunately, there are relatively simple steps you can take to ensure that interested buyers find your auction. Here we've outlined some of the strategies employed by PowerSellers.

Marketing within eBay

There are several options for marketing within eBay; some are formal services offered by eBay and others are strategic. Below are some of the most effective services and strategies that can boost traffic to your eBay Store and auctions.

Timing Your Auctions

An auction is most visible when it is in its final few minutes. eBay's listing sort order defaults to "Time: ending soonest," and therefore the auctions with the least time left rise to the top of the page. Most buyers never bother to resort the listing to anything other than the default, and therefore the overwhelming majority of bidders who see your auction see it in its final few minutes. So naturally you benefit by aligning those final few minutes of your auction with eBay's peak traffic times. This makes the time when your auction is most visible also the time when there are the most bidders on eBay.

The conventional wisdom, as mentioned in Chapter 5, is that Sundays between 6 P.M. and midnight (EST) are eBay's peak traffic hours. In our own research we learned that more than 50 percent of PowerSellers found Sunday to be the most successful day to end an auction. Monday was a distant second with only 10 percent of the vote.

There are two ways to end an auction during peak hours. You could manually submit your auction during that time and set the auction's duration for seven days. Though, if you have more than a few auctions to submit, this process can be time consuming and slow given the high-traffic on eBay's site during this time. Or you could simply pay eBay the additional 10 cents per listing and schedule your auction to begin during this time slot with a seven-day duration. Also, some of the auction management software we outlined in Chapter 10 allows you to schedule listings. There are fees associated with doing it via these programs, though the more expensive ones integrate the scheduling costs into your monthly fee.

Teaser Auctions

Now that you've got your auction timed to maximize exposure, you can begin guiding traffic into your auction, fixed-price listings, and eBay Store with teaser auctions. A teaser auction is set up just like a regular auction, but using a highly popular item, a low starting price, and cross promotion. The Cross-Promotion tool is available to eBay Store owners and places thumbnails of items you've selected from your store into all of your auctions, thereby advertising your more profitable items to interested bidders. These teaser auctions are designed to show up in the main site's search results listings to capture the attention of bidders traveling eBay's main traffic stream.

You should place a few items that are representative of your store inventory up for auction every week. Think of these as the hooks in the stream. Within these auctions you should not only use the Cross-Promotion tool that eBay provides, but also provide links to your eBay Store a few times

> "I personally try to use auctions as advertising tools to get folks into the store. Typically, I will use an item that is very popular so that the listing will be exposed to a high number of people. Advertise your store in those listings."
>
> —swedeng

somewhere in your description or terms. These auctions, in the beginning, will be your major marketing focus. Refine these important auctions to maximize the number of bidders they bring into your store.

Featured Listings

When you can afford to, take advantage of eBay's Featured Listings promotional tools. These are expensive, but when used with your eBay Store and the Cross-Promotion tool, they are highly effective at driving a lot of bidders to your store and auctions. Always use your best-selling items in these featured auctions, and make sure that the products you've chosen to cross-promote are directly related to the featured auction's item. Bidders will not follow a link to an item in which they have no interest. Also, as these will be your most prominent auctions, be sure to spell check your text, proofread, and double check your photos for clarity and accuracy. It is important that these highly visible auctions reflect your business well.

E-Mail Marketing

Included in your eBay Store subscription is an E-mail Marketing tool that allows your customers to subscribe to your eBay Store newsletter. An e-mail newsletter can be a great way to promote sales, specials, your store, and your auctions. The E-mail Marketing tool lets you manage up to five e-mail lists so you can customize your newsletters to your buyers' specific interests.

By doing business on eBay you will be in constant contact with your customers via e-mail. Even if you choose not to use your eBay Store E-mail Marketing tool, it would be a good idea to begin building a database of the e-mail addresses of your customers. Keep careful notes about what each person has purchased from you for appropriate sorting later.

As mentioned earlier, eBay has a strict no-spamming rule that you need to adhere to when putting together e-mail campaigns. You must ask your customers if they would like to subscribe to your mailing list before you begin sending out e-mails, and provide them with a way out if they accept. If you use your eBay Store's E-mail Marketing tool, this will be taken care of for you. You must get permission yourself, however, if you plan to collect and market to e-mail addresses on your own.

Correspondence Promotion

Every time you have contact with a customer, you are presented with an opportunity to do a little promotion. In every package you ship, use eBay's Promotional Flyer tool to print and insert a flyer advertising an upcoming sale or new product line. On every invoice you print, include the address to your eBay Store or make a note about the other popular items you sell. In every e-mail you send out, whether it is a winner confirmation, a payment request, or a post-auction follow-up, include a link to your eBay Store. These simple steps are inexpensive and will help you spread the word about your business in big ways. Always be looking for new promotional ideas.

Marketing Off eBay

Promoting your store and auctions in places other than eBay can be worth your time as well. It is important to promote this business as you would any other. In order to reach the top level among eBay sellers, you must incorporate some of the following methods of promotion.

Your Own Web Site

Many successful PowerSellers have their own web sites. Some use them as complete e-commerce sites separate from eBay, but most find that juggling inventories for two sites is more trouble than it is worth. Your own web site, whether you choose to sell items from it or not, can be a valuable promotional tool for your eBay auctions and store.

A simple independent web site that advertises your eBay Store can open up your business to the millions of users that would otherwise never see your business. eBay offers affiliate tools that allow you to create and customize item listings for inclusion into other web sites via a simple cut-and-paste piece of code. This can be an effective way to direct traffic from non-eBay sources right to your products. And by sending customers directly from search engines to your web site to your eBay Store, you can cleverly route them right past all your eBay competition.

The eBay affiliate tools also allow motivated marketers to create a network of web sites that advertise their products. If you know of any web sites or forums or blogs that would be perfect for advertising your goods, ask them to display an automatically updating affiliate banner showing your products. You will probably have to pay them for this, but the increased traffic could be well worth the expense.

Promotional Programs

Once you have your own web site, you will be able to take advantage of off eBay promotional services such as Google's AdWords program and Overture's marketing tools. These can significantly increase traffic to your web site and to your eBay auctions and store.

As an additional bonus, eBay recognizes that any off eBay promotion of your store that you do also promotes eBay as a whole. Therefore, it offers sellers who market their stores off eBay a 75 percent Final Value Fees discount through the Stores Referral Credit program. See the eBay Stores tutorial pages for more information.

Traditional Real-World Advertising

Don't underestimate the power of traditional, real-world advertising strategies. When used in combination with your own independent web site, advertisements in auto enthusiast trade magazines, on public transportation, and in local newspapers can be quite effective. Advertise your products and web address just as you would any other "real" business; after all, you have a real business. You'll be attracting market segments that most eBay sellers, and internet businesses in general, rarely think to reach out to.

CHAPTER 12

Inventory **Management**

There are two ways to handle the items you sell on eBay. You can purchase the items outright and stock them in your warehouse or storage facility, or you can avoid handling inventory altogether by finding sources that offer drop-shipping. In this chapter, we'll discuss the benefits of both methods so that you can decide which is best for you before you get started.

Drop-Shipping

Drop-shipping is a shipping option that some manufacturers, retailers, and distributors offer to resellers to streamline the selling process. Resellers that use drop-shipping never touch their products.

Instead, they simply notify the shipping department at the item's source company when an item is purchased and the item is shipped directly from the source to the customer. This leaves the reseller free to deal with marketing, auction management, customer service, and payment collection without having to set up inventory management or a shipping department.

While drop-shipping may sound like the ideal shipping solution for eBay sellers, it does have significant drawbacks. First and foremost, surrendering control over the shipping of the items you sell puts you entirely at the mercy of the source company. If it runs out of stock, is delayed in shipping, or even fails to ship an item, it will be quite a difficult process for you to get things straightened out with the company and then make things right with your customer.

Second, the number of companies that offer drop-shipping is limited, which limits your options of what to sell. Your decision about what items to sell should be based on profitability and popularity, not on available shipping options.

Finally, if your product line consists of items from only one or two sources and both sources offer drop-shipping, then it might not be a bad idea for you to take advantage of it. If you seek to expand your product line in the future, however, you could end up trying to manage drop-shipments from ten or more companies. This can grow to become so unwieldy and unmanageable that the thought of centralizing all your products and shipments in your own single warehouse may begin to appeal to you.

Taking on Inventory

If you've decided that drop-shipping isn't your cup of tea, then you've got some planning ahead of you. The first step is finding the finances to make the initial investment in inventory. The second step is finding a storage or warehouse location that meets your needs. Third, you will need to put together a comprehensive strategy for taking care of all your new goodies.

Proper inventory management is essential to any eBay seller's business. When buying and selling thousands of items per week, tracking inventory from source to shelves to shipment can be a monumental task. Many eBay businesses experience growing pains in this area because as their sales increase, they neglect to upgrade their internal inventory management and end up selling items twice, shipping items that haven't sold, and even selling items they haven't yet purchased. These mistakes disappoint customers and quickly tarnish otherwise radiant feedback ratings. Before you start stocking your shelves, be sure that the inventory management strategy you have in place is sufficient for your current needs and will grow along with you.

Space Concerns

Your inventory storage facility must be large enough to hold your inventory comfortably, have a shipping department and a photography area, store extra shipping supplies, and allow room for growth. If you plan to sell just a few items a month, this space might be only as large as the corner of your dining room. Many first-rate eBay businesses have started this way. However, as soon as you begin to develop regular sales, you'll need a facility more suited to your business needs.

Many auto parts have special needs. They can be highly sensitive to their environment, and must therefore be stored in a dry space with relatively ambient temperatures and plenty of shelf space. Some business owners choose self-storage units because they offer security, climate control, and a low initial expense. However, they can sometimes be difficult to access after business hours, and don't leave much room for growth. They also often don't allow you to schedule regular shipping pickups from UPS or FedEx.

If you live in the city or suburbs, look around the industrial parks in your area. You may be able to rent a garage bay with ideal shipping capabilities for not too much more money than a self-storage unit. Low-rent "behind-the-scenes" business parks make ideal locations for eBay businesses. If you are in a rural location, look for some space in a local barn or warehouse.

Software

In Chapter 10 we outlined some auction management programs. All of these programs will help you track your auctions, from listing to sale to feedback. Some of them, such as ChannelAdvisor Pro, will also help you track the flow of your inventory. A good program will notify you when stock of a particular item is running low, relist or restock items that failed to sell at auction, and track your item sources and source expenses.

Layout

If you have the luxury of laying out the floor plan of your storage facility, take "flow" into consideration. The best spaces allow for a continuous stream of inventory through the various stages of handling: logging new inventory, testing (if necessary), photography, shelving, and shipping.

If you have two bay doors, make one "in" for incoming inventory from your item sources, and one "out" for shipments to customers. If you have only one bay door, send all incoming item shipments directly to a processing area where they can be logged into the management software, assigned an inventory ID code, and checked for accuracy and damage. Next, if you're dealing with used inventory, shuffle it all to your testing area where you can make sure everything functions properly and is free of damage. Then, pass everything on to photography so

> "The majority of our items are shipped with UPS. All items are double-boxed so that the customer doesn't receive a damaged item after their wait. We do ship internationally, and use the USPS when we do. The post office is more affordable, and requires less paperwork for both us and the person receiving the product."
>
> —techchoiceparts

> "The shipping method we use depends on the size of the item and where it is going. Large items being shipped domestically usually go UPS. Smaller items usually USPS, and anything going international or off the mainland (to Hawaii or Alaska) also goes USPS."
>
> —truckpartsaz

that the photos you will need to use in your auctions can be taken. If your auction management software doesn't already do this for you, create a photo database to keep track of which photos correspond with what items. For this purpose, have a networked computer set up at the photography station to make the job of listing auctions easier later. Once everything is photographed, you can stock it on your storage shelves while it awaits auction. Label your shelving system and stock your items according to the inventory ID that each item has been assigned, or by using a similar cataloging system, so that when it comes time to ship an item, it will be easily located. Once an item has sold, send it off to the shipping department, and out the "out" door to the happy customer.

Managing a warehouse like this could be enough work for a team of people. Yet many eBay sellers must make do with a lot less manpower. To further organize the process and maximize the work of one or two people, many PowerSellers assign a specific task to different days of the week. For example, on Sunday they devote the day to creating and submitting new auctions to eBay. On Monday, to ensure fast shipping to the customers, they pack and ship all the items that have sold in the auctions that ended on Sunday. On Tuesday, they search for, and purchase, their inventory from the usual sources. On Wednesday, they log in and check all the new inventory shipments that have arrived at the warehouse since the previous Wednesday. On Thursday, they do the necessary photography, and on Friday they stock the items on the warehouse shelves. Saturday might be a day off, but it is more likely to be a day spent doing everything they couldn't finish up during the week. Of course, this schedule makes for a hectic week, but on the bare-bones budget of a new business, sometimes it is necessary.

> "We ship UPS within the United States. Most of the time UPS is good, but, as with anything, they have their frustrating moments. We also ship USPS when we ship to places like Alaska, Hawaii, or Europe."
>
> —swedeng

Shipping Choices

There are three main companies that sellers choose to handle their shipping: UPS, FedEx, or the U.S. Postal Service (USPS). You will have to research which company works best in your area and location. The USPS tends to be the least expensive, but you'll need to deliver packages to the post office every time you ship. UPS and FedEx are a little pricier, but will come to your door and pick up shipments. All three provide tracking numbers for your packages, which buyers always appreciate having.

When shipping internationally, be sure to fill out all the appropriate customs forms from whichever shipping company you choose.

CHAPTER 13

Finances

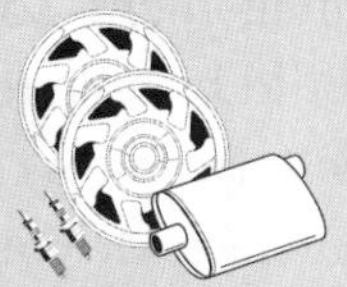

With the possibility of hundreds of transactions per month, you will need to be diligent about tracking and recording your business's finances. Solid accounting practices will help you not only come tax time, but also with securing a bank loan, evaluating the health of your business, and selling the company when that time comes.

There are several ways to manage your business's finances. You can do it yourself, either by hand or by using accounting software, or you can hire an accountant to help you. If you're confident in your bookkeeping skills and have the time and energy to take on the task yourself, then by all means, do it. Don't take on your own bookkeeping, however, if you are not sure of yourself, don't have adequate time to do the job, or are just trying to save a few bucks. Doing a lousy job of bookkeeping will no doubt cost you more in the end than simply hiring an accountant up front.

Doing It Yourself

If you decide to take on the job yourself, you can find good help in the form of accounting software. There are a few great programs available that are designed to do exactly what you need. Luckily, if you accept most of your payments from buyers through PayPal, you will have easy access to a downloadable record of your received payments, which you can plug into the accounting software you choose. Also, if your auction management software allows you to track inventory, you should be able to export a list of all your inventory purchases. These two lists combine to compile a record of your business's finances. All you need to do is fill in around the edges with information such as your office and shipping expenses, income received from outside (non-PayPal) sources, rent, and utilities.

Research the programs below before you decide which one to use. Some have downloadable demo versions that will allow you to evaluate the software for a period of time.

QuickBooks

Perhaps most well-known is the business accounting program QuickBooks, from Intuit, the makers of Quicken. QuickBooks is available for both Macs and Window PCs, costs between $100 and $400 depending on the version, and releases an upgrade every year to stay current with tax information. For more information, visit www.quickbooks.com.

Money Small Business

Microsoft's Money Small Business is another widely used financial management application. It will help you manage your accounts, spending, and profit and loss reports through a simple interface. Money only runs on PCs running Windows XP or higher and costs around $90. For more information, visit www.microsoft.com/money/.

PeachTree

PeachTree's small business accounting software has been around and popular for many years. It is a robust accounting program specifically designed for small businesses. Like Money, it only operates on Windows PCs. It costs $199.95 and comes out in a new version every year. For more information, visit www.peachtree.com.

Business Vital Signs

The most important aspect of doing your own bookkeeping is to actually do it. Saving all your receipts and invoices for a rainy day during tax season will not help you to produce the quarterly, monthly, and weekly reports that you will need to make smart business decisions. You should be aware at all times of your company's vital signs, as indicated by your profit and loss statement, cash flow statement, and balance sheet.

Your profit and loss statement (P&L) should be studied every month and can likely be produced from within your accounting software. It is simply a record of all your income and expenses over a given time period, usually a month. It will let you know whether your business is profitable and, if not, where you need to make changes. Keep a file of previous months' P&Ls so that you can compare and track whether or not the changes you've made are working.

A cash flow statement simply tracks the money that comes into and goes out of your business. It can be used to track where your cash has gone, and to predict where your cash will be down the road. You should create a cash flow statement often so that you are never sideswiped by surprises. You need to know that you will have enough cash available to purchase next month's inventory. Otherwise, you'll be left with nothing to sell and no income.

A balance sheet measures all your assets (inventory, vehicles, cash, accounts receivable, etc.) against all your liabilities (loans, rent, accounts payable, etc.) and determines what your business is worth. Keeping a close eye on this report will let you know if your business is growing, or headed for failure. Generate this often for early signs of trouble.

Finding Help

You have quite enough to stay on top of, without trying to remain current on, all the latest tax laws. Your time will be better spent watching for trends and innovations on eBay than watching for the latest IRS tax codes. Accountants can relieve you of a lot of stress, and therefore you should consider passing your accounting on to one of them.

Talk to other local businesses to find out who they trust for their accounting. If that search turns up empty, talk to your local SCORE chapter, area chamber of commerce, or state Small Business Association for recommendations. You'll want to interview several accountants before you enlist the help of one. Be sure to inquire into her work history. Has she been in the profession long? Is she a Certified Public Accountant? How much experience does she have accounting for small businesses? Solicit resumes. Ask for references. And then follow through on calling them all. Your business will profit from your diligent research.

CHAPTER 14

Human Resources

The day will come when it is necessary for you to start hiring employees. This chapter will discuss how to know when that day has arrived and what steps to take when it does. It will be a busy day, no doubt, and you likely will feel stressed and anxious about taking the time to find help amid your already hectic schedule. But take a deep breath and relax. This is a necessary and exciting step to building a business. Once you've got good employees behind you, your business will really start to take off.

When to Hire

Running an eBay business takes a lot of work. It requires long hours in front of a computer screen, a lot of time on the phone, and some

> "During our busy seasons, spring and summer, we employ ten people. During the slower months, we cut that down to about five key people."
>
> —techchoicepart

stressful financial decisions. It is indeed a full-time job. But it should only be a full-time job. When the number of hours you work in a week creeps past 40 to 50 to 60 and worse, you should consider hiring some help. Remember, you started this eBay business to have more fun, take control of your schedule, and free up some time. Didn't you?

If you find yourself working more than 40 hours a week to keep up with the demands of the business, you should be in a position financially to afford one or two part-time employees. If you're not in a position to take on a few salaries, you should reassess the profitability of your business. Would it be more profitable to run fewer auctions at higher prices? Or would the extra help be all that you needed to increase sales and cover the salaries? In either case, you should speak with your accountant about taking on help. He will be able to help you determine how much you can afford to pay, and whether or not you should offer benefits.

Before You Hire

Prior to hiring employees there are things you must do. New employees means new planning and new paperwork. The first step before you hire is to get yourself set up properly with the government.

Employer Identification Number

Up until this point, if you have operated your business as a sole proprietorship, you have not needed an employer identification number (EIN). An EIN is to a business what a social security number is to an individual. It simply identifies your business to the IRS and is used when you withhold income taxes from your employees' paychecks. To apply for your EIN, you will need to fill out and submit IRS Form SS-4. It can be downloaded from www.irs.gov/pub/irs-pdf/fss4.pdf.

Planning for Employees

Before you begin interviewing you should figure out where another set of hands would be most effective. What is the most time-consuming task in your day? Is it easily delegated to someone else or does it require your expertise? If you find yourself spending six hours a day shipping orders, you might consider hiring someone to take that on and free yourself up to generate more income for the business. Your time is best spent working on your business, not in it.

A helpful tool you can create is an employee map of your business. Draw out a job tree, placing yourself at the top as the boss. Below you, sketch the branches of your company: auction management, customer service, accounting, inventory management, shipping, and others. Within the branches, map out the individual jobs that you would need to make each branch run effectively. For each job you've mapped out, write a clear job description.

It may be years before your business is able to fill all the positions you've planned. But now is the time to begin hiring. Start with the jobs that can be easily filled and would most effectively free up your time. Then work toward filling the ones that aren't as crucial but would make everything run more smoothly. In the beginning, you may need to hire one person for a few positions. But because you've already written clear job descriptions, you can simply hand your new employee two or three descriptions and divide his week up accordingly.

Finding Employees

Finding people to apply for the positions you've created might be the easiest step in the whole process. Place an ad in your local papers, talk to friends and relatives, and put up fliers at the mall. Once you begin advertising your position, applicants will come find you. Be aware of the markets in which you're advertising. If you're looking for an accountant, fliers at the mall will likely not yield legitimate results. If you're looking for a teenager to help part time with auction listings, advertising accordingly.

Screening Applicants

One of the largest problem areas for small business owners is troublesome employees. This is your chance to do all you can to weed out potentially troublesome employees before you begin hiring. In addition to accepting the standard employment application—available at any local office supply store—make sure you also check references, get proof of citizenship, conduct interviews, and do background checks. Hiring help will do nothing for your business if you end up with a thief in the middle of your stock room. Conversely, hiring the right people now may be exactly what your business needs to grow to the next level.

After You Hire

Now that you've got employees, your business is ready to roll. Or is it? There are still a few concerns that need your attention. Simply filling positions will not help a company run. Now you need to make sure your employees know what to do, and you need to know what to do to take care of them.

More Paperwork

In addition to keeping each new employee's application, resume (if submitted), and references on file, you need to collect tax information from them. As the employer, you will be withholding income tax on your employee's paychecks. The amount you withhold is determined by the information your employee fills out on his or her Form W-4. You will need to keep a copy of Form W-4, and mail one off to the IRS.

You must also ask your new employee to fill out Form I-9, the Employment Eligibility Verification. To do this you will need a copy of the employee's passport, or driver's license and social security card. For a complete list of acceptable forms of identification, see the back of Form I-9. You must keep every employee's Form I-9 on file for a period of three years from the hiring date. This form is not mailed to anyone.

Training

Spending time training your new employee thoroughly may seem like a pain and distraction now, but it will pay off in the long run. It is easier to train an employee well in the first two weeks than it is to be asked to help them every few minutes for six months. Provide your employee with the detailed job description you wrote out at the beginning of this process. She will find it a useful guide when she has questions.

Taxes

FEDERAL INCOME TAX. As mentioned above, you need to withhold federal income taxes from your employees on every paycheck. The appropriate amount to withhold is determined by the tax information the individual employee supplies on the Form W-4. Use this information to find the appropriate amount in IRS Publication 15, Circular E, *Employer's Tax Guide*.

FICA. In addition to federal income tax, you must also withhold Social Security and Medicare taxes from each employee's check and pay a matching amount. At the time of this writing, the Social Security tax rate was 6.2 percent for all salaries up to $76,000, and 1.45 percent for Medicare.

FUTA. FUTA stands for the Federal Unemployment Tax Act, and it means that you need to pay more money. You pay 6.2 percent of the first $7,000 that your employee earns. However, you receive a credit for 5.4 percent of that on your own taxes. Use Form 940 or Form 940-EZ to file these taxes.

EMPLOYEE COMPENSATION. Along with all the paperwork above, you must submit to the IRS a report of employee compensation and withholdings, along with your share of the FICA taxes, on Form 941, *Employer's Quarterly Federal Tax Return*.

When you apply for your EIN, the IRS will send you many copies of Form 8109, the Federal Tax Deposit Coupon. If your total quarterly employment taxes are more than $500, you will need to file these taxes using Form 8109 every month before the 15th of the following month.

At the end of the year you will need to provide your employees with their annual Form W-2s. This form, as I'm sure you know, summarizes earnings and withholdings for the year. You must deliver this form to all your employees before January 31st of the following year. You will need to keep a copy of all your employees' Form W-2s to file along with Form W-3 to the Social Security Administration.

Yes, that's a lot of effort, math, and paperwork. For these reasons, many companies fill the accountant position first. If you find yourself stuck or confused by these tax requirements, you can do your own research at the following web sites:

- Social Security Administration (www.ssa.gov)
- Internal Revenue Service (www.irs.gov)
- Small Business Administration (www.sba.gov)

Or, you can find someone to help you at these sites:

- 1-800-Accountant (www.1800accountant.com)
- CPA Directory (www.cpadirectory.com)
- The National Association of Small Business Accountants (www.smallbizaccountants.com)

CHAPTER 15

Final **Thoughts**

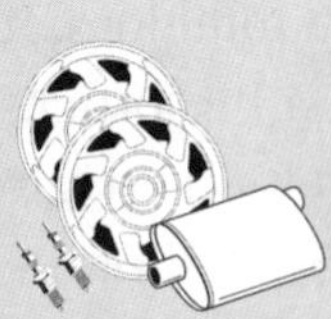

Well, there you have it—a crash course in selling auto parts on eBay. You now know how to register on eBay, find items to sell, create effective auctions, manage inventory, and hire help when it's time. We've provided you with the best strategies for getting started, and the proven techniques for maximizing profitability. Now it's up to you to become the next successful PowerSeller in the world's largest marketplace.

Remember, selling on eBay will not always be easy. But you have chosen to do it because selling auto parts is a fun way of life. That in itself makes this venture more rewarding than any dead-end corporate job anywhere. You have taken the reigns of your income and opened up your future to possibilities as limitless as eBay has proven, so far, to be. In time, you will learn more ins and outs of this marketplace than we could ever stuff into a pocket guide. I hope this book has been able to set you on the right path to building a profitable and enjoyable business selling auto parts.

As most sellers will tell you, there's more to eBay than profits, e-mail, and inventory. People do it for many reasons, most of which are more meaningful than you would expect. Here are some closing thoughts about selling on eBay from some of our PowerSellers.

PowerSeller sumofallparts started selling on eBay with one wrecked motorcycle and the hope that the bike wouldn't be a total loss. Just five years later, the owners' goals for eBay are a bit loftier. The sellers aim to "develop a rock-solid system for managing inventory and developing product, scale up to $1 million per month in sales, and sell the business to an investment group." We applaud them on their success and wish them the best in the future.

Similarly, mvp-imports started selling on eBay with just a few Volvo headlights. Now, thanks to hard work by these sellers and the massive reach of eBay, they are on track to achieving their goal "to be the number-one seller of Volvo lighting products in the world."

"eBay lets us, as a smaller company have a much larger, even global, market," says Greg Macintosh of techchoiceparts.

"Our local market is rather crowded with businesses with similar products. Being on eBay, we have a much larger presence in the marketplace." The goals of techchoiceparts are a bit more humble than those of the first two PowerSellers. Macintosh puts it like this: "Obviously our first goal is to make millions! That aside, I hope we can continue to profit, while helping consumers get quality products at affordable prices. One of the best feelings to have is when someone calls or e-mails and thanks me for saving her money over everywhere else she looked. Our final goal is to be the number one seller in our eBay category by providing top-notch service and quality."

Crystal Conway of swedeng is as excited about eBay as we are. She had this to say: "eBay is the greatest advertising tool known to man. Word of mouth cannot travel as fast as the internet. Everyone knows eBay. Even people who have never touched a keyboard and think that the internet is some place on Lake Erie, still know eBay."

I thank the PowerSellers who took the time to participate in this book, and wish them, and you, success in the largest buying and selling community in the world. We hope you are inspired by the potential eBay possesses for you and your future business ventures.

The eBay Community Values:

- We believe people are basically good.
- We believe everyone has something to contribute.
- We believe that an honest, open environment can bring out the best in people.

- We recognize and respect everyone as a unique individual.
- We encourage you to treat others the way you want to be treated.

Good luck to you in your new adventure.

APPENDIX

Resource **Guide**

eBay's Useful Tools

eBay's Solutions Directory

http://solutions.ebay.com

This directory contains applications and services from both eBay and non-eBay developers that help eBay buyers and sellers manage interactions with eBay. It is the most comprehensive eBay tools directory on the internet, complete with a rating system measuring the quality of each application or service.

eBay's Marketplace Research

http://pages.ebay.com/marketplace_research/

Marketplace Research is a service that eBay provides to help sellers collect information about the sales histories and trends of items and categories.

eBay's Reviews and Guides
http://reviews.ebay.com/
This directory contains user-submitted reviews of items and guides for eBay buying and selling tactics. Each guide is reviewed and rated by other eBayers for quality of information.

eBay's Want It Now
http://pages.ebay.com/wantitnow/
Want It Now allows people seeking specific items that cannot currently be found on eBay to post a request for the items where other eBayers can see what's in demand. Sellers can browse the Want It Now postings to gauge what items are in demand, and to possibly supply a requested item to the requester.

eBay's Wholesale Lots
http://pages.ebay.com/catindex/catwholesale.html
Sellers with stock to get rid of, or stock to buy, use eBay's Wholesale Lots site to buy and sell whole lots of items.

eBay's Business Marketplace
http://pages.ebay.com/businessmarketplace/index.html
eBay's Business Marketplace deals in business-specific items, such as office technology, supplies, industrial equipment, and professional audio/video/photography equipment. Sellers can find good deals on shipping materials, extra computers, software, and more.

eBay Pulse
http://pulse.ebay.com/
eBay Pulse provides a cursory glance over the popular items in each category of eBay. It is not very useful to serious sellers, and should not be relied upon for product research. It is, however, interesting to browse to satisfy casual category curiosity.

Skype
www.skype.com
Skype is eBay's VoIP (voice-over-internet-protocol) and IM (instant messaging) program. When integrated into an auction page, it allows sellers to speak to buyers all around the world for free if the buyer is also using Skype, or for a low per-minute rate if the buyer is using a regular telephone.

Useful Third-Party Tools

Terapeak Marketplace Research
www.terapeak.com
Terapeak is a popular eBay research tool. Sellers use Terapeak to assess the likely final sale price of their items, judge the best time of day and week to end auctions, watch eBay item and category trends, and find new items.

Terapeak Motors P&A Research
www.terapeak.com/ebay_motors_research/
Terapeak Motors is the only eBay Motors-exclusive research tool. It provides sellers with item selling history and information for cars, auto parts, and accessories.

HammerTap

www.hammertap.com

HammerTap is an eBay research software suite featuring licensed eBay data. It is designed to help sellers find products that sell, list more successful auctions, maximize profits, and anticipate selling costs.

dealer123

www.dealer123.com

dealer123 is an eBay Motors item listing tool. It makes the tasks associated with listing automobile-related items easier, such as displaying information from CARFAX or AutoCheck, generating inspection reports, and photo management.

Glossary

About Me. A page you can create on eBay that tells other members about you and your eBay business. You'll see the About Me icon next to the User ID of anyone who has an About Me page. Click on the icon to view that person's page.

Auction-style listing (online auction format). The basic, most common way to sell an item on eBay—listing the item for sale, collecting bids for a fixed length of time, and selling the item to the winning bidder.

Bid cancellation. The cancellation of a bid by a seller during an auction.

Bid increment. The amount by which a bid must be raised in order for it to be accepted in an auction-style listing.

Bid retraction. The cancellation of a bid by a buyer during an auction-style listing.

Bidder search. A search for all the items that a member of eBay has placed bids on.

Block bidders/buyers. A feature that lets you create a list of specific eBay members who are not allowed to bid on or buy items you list for sale. A person on the list will be blocked from participating in all of your items until you take them off the list. You may want to do this if you've had a negative experience with a buyer in the past.

Buy It Now (BIN). A listing feature that lets a buyer purchase an item immediately for a price the seller has set.

Category listings. The set of categories by which items are organized on eBay.

Dispute Console. The Dispute Console helps buyers and sellers manage, track, and take action on disputes related to their transactions. Accessible through My eBay, the Dispute Console is used for the Unpaid Item Process and the Item Not Received Process.

eBay time. The official time of day at eBay headquarters in San Jose, California in the United States. This location is in the Pacific time zone.

Feedback. A system that eBay members use to rate their buying or selling experience with another eBay member. This helps keep eBay a safe place to buy and sell. After a listing is completed, the buyer and seller can leave a rating (positive, neutral, or negative) and a comment about each other. These become a permanent part of a member's profile and can be viewed by the rest of the eBay Community. To see a member's full feedback profile, click on the number in parentheses next to their User ID. The feedback system helps you build your reputation on eBay and helps you check the reputation of other members of the community.

Final value fee. A fee eBay charges to a seller when a listing ends. This fee is based on the "final value" of the item, which is the closing bid or sale price. Please note that currently, eBay Singapore is not charging sellers any fees.

Fixed price format. A selling format that lets you list an item for an unchanging, set price, with no auction-style bidding.

Member profile. A page showing all of a member's feedback information, including ratings and comments from others who have bought or sold with that person before.

My eBay. A central place on eBay where you can manage all of your activities, including buying, selling, feedback, and general account preferences.

Online auction format (auction-style listing). The basic, most common way to sell an item on eBay—listing the item for sale, collecting bids for a fixed length of time, and selling the item to the highest bidder.

PayPal. A fast, easy, secure payment method offered by many eBay sellers for purchasing items.

PowerSeller. A seller on eBay who has maintained a 98 percent positive feedback score and provided a high level of service to their buyers.

Proxy bidding. The feature of an auction-style listing in which eBay automatically bids on your behalf, up to the maximum amount you set.

Relisting. Listing an item for sale again after it did not sell the first time.

Reserve price. Setting a reserve price lets you start the bidding at a price lower than you would be willing to sell for. If the highest bid does not meet your reserve price, then you're under no obligation to sell the item to the bidder.

Second chance offer. A feature that lets you make an offer to a nonwinning bidder when either the winning bidder has failed to pay for your item, or you have a duplicate of the item.

Sell similar item. A feature that lets you list a new item based on the information you've previously entered for another item. When you choose this option, eBay automatically transfers information from the old listing into the new one for easy editing. You save time by not having to enter the same information again.

Seller's return policy. A feature in the Sell Your Item form that enables sellers to specify their product return policy. This feature includes a set of preformatted policies from which the seller can choose. Once the seller chooses a return policy, it appears in a corresponding section of the View Item page.

Seller search. A search for a specific seller on eBay.

Selling manager. An advanced eBay selling tool that lets you perform all of your listing and sales-related activities from one location in My eBay.

Shill bidding. The deliberate placing of bids to artificially raise the price of an item. This practice undermines trust in the eBay Community and is not permitted.

Sniping. Placing a bid in the closing minutes or seconds of an auction-style listing.

Starting price. The price at which you want bidding for your item to begin in an auction-style listing.

Store inventory format. A selling format that eBay Store sellers can use to list items in their store for a fixed price.

Title search. A method of finding items on eBay by entering keywords that match the title of the items.

TurboLister. An advanced eBay selling tool that helps you create multiple eBay listings quickly and easily offline on your computer.

Unpaid item process. The dispute resolution process used by sellers when they have not been paid for their item.

Common eBay Auction Title Abbreviations

$1LR	One dollar, low reserve
$1NR	One dollar, no reserve
AI/WI	As-is, where is
AO	All original
BIN	Buy It Now
BNIB	Brand new in box
BNWL	Brand new with labels
BNWOT	Brand new without tags
BNWT	Brand new with tags
EX	Excellent condition
G/GD	Good condition
HTF	Hard to find
Imp.	Imported
ITF	Impossible to find
LE	Limited edition
Liq.	Liquidation

LN	Like new
LOT	Group of multiple items sold together as a "lot"
LTD	Limited edition
MNT	Mint. In perfect condition (a subjective term)
MIB	Mint in box
MIJ	Made in Japan
MIMB	Mint in mint box
MIMP	Mint in mint package
MIP	Mint in package
MNB	Mint no box
MOC	Mint on card
MOMC	Mint on mint card
MWBT	Mint with both tags
MWMT	Mint with mint tags
NBU	Never been used
NIB	New in box
NR	No reserve
NS	No shipping
NW	Not worn/never worn/needs work
NWT	New with tags
OEM	Original equipment manufacturer
OOAK	One of a kind
OOP	Out of print/out of production

PP	PayPal
Ref.	Refurbished
RIB	Refurbished in box
SBO	Serious bidders only
SH/S&H	Shipping and handling
SHI	Shipping, handling, and insurance
SIB	Sealed in box
Unt.	Untested
VF	Very fine
VG	Very good
Vint.	Vintage
w/	"with"
Wty.	Includes warranty

Index